Praise for *Missed Translations*

"Sopan Deb hilariously and truthfully lets us in on the ups, downs, lefts, and rights of trying to understand—as a stand-up comedian and a journalist—the two grown-up strangers who raised him. It's a crazy story, but you know: Good crazy. Funny crazy. Read-this-book crazy."

—**PETE HOLMES**, comedian, podcast host, and author of *Comedy Sex God*

"Sopan Deb taps into both the darkness and light that permeate a story about love, family, and understanding. He's a masterful storyteller, and I'm thankful for his bravery and willingness to share the kind of human story that we too often prefer to keep to ourselves."

—**KAL PENN**, actor, writer, and producer

"Both moving and hilarious, Missed Translations is not just about exploring culture, family, and love, but about understanding where one comes from in the deepest possible way. It's a wonderful journey."

—**JAKE TAPPER**, Chief Washington Correspondent for CNN and author of *The Hellfire Club*

"As a man who has both been a performer and covered performance, Sopan Deb now paints his most important picture yet, the self-portrait."

—**ROY WOOD JR.**, comedian and correspondent on The Daily Show with Trevor Noah

AF658565

"A sympathetic portrait of South Asians who are neither crazy and rich nor humorless nerds...Memoirs by children of immigrants often fault clueless parents; this one is refreshing for Deb's realization that—whatever his elders' missteps—he needed "to take some responsibility for my part in our family's disconnect" for things to change."

— ***KIRKUS REVIEWS***

"While his topic is serious, Deb's writing is breezy and witty, and his earnestness will sweep readers up into this charmer of a memoir."

— ***BOOKLIST***

"A delightful memoir of people and place that will draw in Deb's fans and attract plenty of new ones."

—***LIBRARY JOURNAL*** (starred review)

Missed Translations

MISSED TRANSLATIONS

MEETING THE INDIAN PARENTS
WHO RAISED ME

SOPAN DEB

SIMON &
SCHUSTER

London • New York • Sydney • Toronto • New Delhi

A VIACOM CBS COMPANY

First published in HarperCollins Publishers,
195 Broadway, New York, NY 10007.

Published in India by Simon & Schuster India, 2020
A Vaicom CBS company

Copyright © 2020 by Sopan Deb.

All rights reserved.

No part of this book may be reproduced in any form or by any means, electronic or mechanical, including photography, recording, or by any information storage and retrieval system or technologies now known or later developed, without permission in writing from the publisher.

ISBN 978-81-947520-1-1 ebook ISBN 978-81-947520-3-5

Printed and bound in India by Replika Press Pvt. Ltd.

MIX
Paper from responsible sources
FSC® C016779

Simon & Schuster India is committed to sourcing paper that is made from wood grown in sustainable forests and support the Forest Stewardship Council,® the leading international forest certification organisation.

Our books displaying the FS ®C logo are printed on FSC® certified paper.
No part of this publication may be reproduced, transmitted or stored in a retrieval system, in any form or by any means, electronic, mechanical, photocopying, recording or otherwise, without the prior permission of the publisher.

This book is sold subject to the condition that it shall not, by way of trade or otherwise, be lent, resold, hired out, or otherwise circulated, without the publisher's prior consent, in any form of binding or cover other than that in which it is published.

To Wesley, my rock and partner,
without whom none of this would have happened

CONTENTS

AUTHOR'S NOTE

When I first considered reaching out to my parents, I thought of chronicling the process as a documentary. But I felt that cameras would be too intrusive for comfort and instead opted to write it all down, each step of the way. I wanted to give the reader the same experience of unfolding discovery I had as I navigated through this tumultuous journey.

This book is a collection of true stories, some remembered but mostly recorded over the course of roughly a year between 2018 and 2019. Extensive interviews, photos, video, audio, professional fact-checking, and ancient Gchat histories have been used to piece it all together in as precise a manner as possible. As you'll see, dates and even a person's age or number of siblings sometimes ultimately required an estimate. Most quotes you'll read are verbatim from my own recordings. The others the result of copious note-taking in the moment or recall from my childhood. A small number of quotes and conversations were edited for clarity.

I want to note that each member of the Deb family has their own version of this tale, which mirrors my memory in some cases and contradicts it in others. Some stories, particularly those based on recall and those that took place well before I was born, were impossible to verify. To the best of my ability, I gave my mother and father space to tell their stories in these pages, but the final product is my truth alone.

Most important, this is not the story of all those of South Asian descent. This is only my experience. Nor is this a story *only* for those of South Asian descent. I hope everyone can take something from it, whether it's a lesson about comedy, forgiveness, or how to properly send an email.

DIRECTORY OF DEBS

Given the endless supply of "S" names in my family, here's a quick reference guide to keep you oriented.

Sachindra & Binodini
Sopan's paternal grandparents;
Shyamal's parents

Sudhirendra
Shyamal's eldest brother

Namita
Sudhirendra's wife

Somnath
Sudhirendra & Namita's son

Susmita
Somnath's wife

Ron & Trisha
Somnath & Susmita's children

Siddhartha
Shyamal's youngest brother

Meera
Siddhartha's wife

Shyamal
Sopan's father

Amiya & Pravat
Sopan's maternal grandparents;
Bishakha's parents

Atish
Bishakha's brother

Sima
Atish's wife

Sagnik
Atish & Sima's son

Bishakha
Sopan's mother

Sattik
Sopan's older brother

Erica
Sattik's wife

Tessa & Braden
Sattik & Erica's children

Sopan

FOREWORD

By Hasan Minhaj

When Sopan asked me to write this foreword, I was honored. The man has an impressive résumé. He has worked as a journalist for the *Boston Globe*, NBC News, Al Jazeera, and CBS News, where he covered Trump's presidential campaign. He then became a culture writer at the *New York Times*, and now he's on the NBA beat there. I want that job. Watch basketball all day, analyze it, and get paid for it? That's the dream gig. But he's *also* a stand-up comedian. That's the genius move he pulled off—getting an extremely reputable day job that his family understands and can be proud of, and then sneaking comedy into the bottom of his résumé. Brilliant.

Sopan could write about anything, but for him to choose to write about his experiences growing up brown in America to two immigrant parents is special to me. I've always felt that the South Asian diaspora needs more of our stories being told. There are certain mythologies of growing up brown in America that we all share. I see so much of my family in Sopan's story—his father's pride, his mother's stubbornness, his partner's need to be endlessly patient and forgiving. There's so much time spent sitting in living rooms doing nothing. So much time.

His longing to bond with his father over sports, to learn about his parents' siblings, and to make his mom happy by bringing her to a Broadway show are not just immigrant sentiments, but

American ones. His yearning to connect to his family is relatable on so many levels.

Sopan and I had similar upbringings. We're both kids with melanin who grew up in super white towns—Howell, New Jersey, and Davis, California, respectively. We both came of age around the same time. Our parents both had arranged marriages, lived far from home and their families, and learned how to use email waaaaay after it was socially acceptable. I don't know this for sure, but I would guess we both obsessed over the same Air Jordans when we were in high school.

Nevertheless, our individual experiences are unique, nuanced, and worth sharing. But Sopan pushes his story well beyond the typical, "*Hey my parents wanted me to get straight As*" model minority narrative. He dives right into the darkest sides of South Asian culture, stuff that we only see in our living rooms, but never talk about. Depression, divorce, abuse, and betrayal are put front and center. And he does this in the gutsiest way possible: he asks his parents about it to their face.

South Asian families don't talk about their problems. We're expected to tough it out, take a nap, sweep it under the rug, and go back to work. The most therapy most of us received came from illegally downloaded episodes of *The Sopranos* that we watched after everyone else was asleep.

We're not equipped to handle this stuff. But Sopan goes at it head-on, like only a true journalist (and comedian) could. I genuinely hope that this book starts a conversation between family members. We need it. No more lying about our pasts. Who we're dating. Why our parents are unhappy. Why we won't talk about mental health or therapy. He's forced my hand at dealing with these issues. And if all of this is too heavy, at the very least I hope it forces some Indian uncles to tell the truth about how much money they had in their pockets when they first came to America.

PROLOGUE

"Shambo, the thing is that if you do not have peace at home, you can work hard or whatever, but you've got to have someone to come back to," Atish said. "You remember I used to watch my favorite television show, *Cheers*? And there was that song called—"

"You want to go where everybody knows your name, yeah," I interrupted.

"So this is the thing. Where you are comfortable, where you feel good: That's the thing that you guys didn't have. Like if I'm away, as soon as I get out of home, let's say fifteen minutes, I get a phone call. 'Where are you?'" Atish said, looking at Sima, his wife of more than thirty years. "Sometimes I get mad. She always worries about me. But that's the thing: I know inside that I'm wanted. That someone is missing me. Someone wants me home. So that's the thing: You have to have love in your life."

ONE

"I'd like to say a few words about race relations."

I grabbed the mic and locked in. It was January 2018, on the cusp of my thirtieth birthday, and I was prowling back and forth onstage at the Comic Strip Live, a comedy club on New York City's Upper East Side. I was absolutely *killing* it, man. A rare feeling.

Stand-up comedy crowds can be warm. I'm prepared for them to be icy. Used to it, really. But this one was on fire. Bodies were squeezed into every seat just looking for an excuse to laugh. I felt larger than life, like Mario after eating a mushroom or LeBron dunking on a fast break.

The Comic Strip is an institution. Seinfeld. Chappelle. Sandler. Murphy. Rock. Every comic who has *made it* had, at some point, gone through this place. The venue is deep and cavernous, with seats crammed at long tables strewn throughout the room. Behind the stage is a familiar brick wall. Somewhere between the main stage and the front entrance, out of sight of the crowd, is a green room for performers, which is more like a green broom closet. In some parts of the venue, it's hard to see the performer. When you're the one telling jokes, you can't see shit.

My set was part of the *Big Brown Comedy Hour*, a recurring show that Dean Obeidallah and Maysoon Zayid, New York City–based comics, started in 2009 as a way of putting a spotlight on up-and-coming comics of South Asian or Middle Eastern descent. These shows are always packed to the brim with, well, brown people who rarely get to see shows like this. When brown crowds are in, they come to *laugh*.

After seven years of doing comedy, getting the room to laugh because of something I constructed still gives me a high. When a punchline really lands—I mean, *really*—it is the kind of moment I want to freeze, store in a jar, and put on a shelf forever. Or pour into one of those Pensieves from Harry Potter.

But laughter is fleeting, and you have to keep things fresh. That night, I decided to test out some new material—a seasonally appropriate bit about the holidays:

> *My favorite Christmas tradition growing up was asking my mom what the meaning of Christmas was. Every year, we'd be like, "Hey Mom! What's the meaning of Christmas?" She'd go, "Oh, it's when Jesus died on the cross." We'd say, "Oh. Why did Jesus die on the cross?" She'd answer, "It's because Jesus became a carpenter instead of a DOCTOR!"*

The bit played on a tired South Asian trope that Indian kids are supposed to become doctors. It didn't *quite* slay, but I heard the laughter ripple across the room. What I didn't hear was my own bullshit.

For one thing, I grew up Hindu. My family didn't exactly have Christmas traditions, which explains why I confused

Christmas and Easter. The only traditions of any kind we had were family squabbles and seething resentment that split our family into warring factions. What I knew about healthy families at Christmas was what I saw in pop culture. Think "chestnuts roasting on an open fire" or *Miracle on 34th Street* or Tim Allen's *The Santa Clause*. Yes, even the last one.

The best stand-up comics deliver searing honesty to the audience. They're supposed to expose and clarify truths about the world as they see it. They heighten hypocrisies and spotlight inequalities, and they do it all for the crowd's amusement. Someone once framed it for me this way: The greats tell the audience what is funny rather than try to make them laugh.

But I was handing this crowd *someone else's* honesty with that joke, telling them what I pictured a stereotypical Christmas with Indian parents to be like. That I didn't know the first thing about a happy Christmas made me all the more eager to talk about it. It was a paradox: I had spent much of my life running away from my skin color and culture, and yet the thing I felt most comfortable discussing onstage was my South Asian ethnicity. Talking about any version of the brown experience felt cathartic, whether it was the mangled one of my childhood or the way I imagined a happy brown kid growing up.

I had just ten minutes to give the crowd at the Comic Strip a little taste of *my* truth, and I had more to say. I launched into some jokes I had written about *my* Indian family. This was the real stuff. First, there was the bitter divorce between my mother, Bishakha, and my father, Shyamal, after a long and ill-fated arranged marriage. Then there was a healthy dose of cultural alienation, a smattering of outlandish (but totally true) stories about my parents, and the father who disappeared to India eleven years prior without telling anyone. No, really. He did.

I had the punchlines down pat.

I love family reunions. Anybody here been to a good family reunion?

When I do this bit, nobody ever raises their hands. It gives me a beat to take stock of the audience before inquiring:

Is this a room of fucking orphans?

That gets a chuckle, but it's just the amuse-bouche. A warm-up for the appetizer.

I, for one, really love family reunions. Mine are typically in court.

It's a good, not great, joke. I like it, though. If jokes are comedians' children, that one would be Cindy Brady: Fine, it gets the job done, but who really cares? The audience at the Comic Strip agreed. A solid Cindy.

But what the crowd never knew, and what I couldn't bring myself to tell them, was the crippling anxiety and sadness I felt about each of the truths I had morphed into a laugh line. I was comfortable talking about this stuff from behind a microphone, but only to an extent. Sometimes it felt like I was playing the part of a brown guy onstage, but when I dropped the façade and delved into my actual life, the words deflected the guilt and vulnerability I wasn't yet ready to face. Much of my material—especially the stuff about my parents—resulted from unfamiliarity, both with myself and with them.

Look, stand-up comedy is a mostly masochistic endeavor. That's why I have a day job as a writer for the *New York Times*. The *Times* gig is a fantastic outlet for curiosity and for exploring the humanity of others. I can interview other people and probe them with questions I might not be able to ask of myself. As for comedy, I'm only willing to flagellate myself for free and after hours.

At the time of this set in January 2018, I hadn't seen my mother or father in years. My relationship with each of them had its own contours but essentially landed in the same place: I considered them distant footnotes from my past. At that moment, I wasn't entirely sure where either parent was living.

When I started writing this book, right after the *Big Brown* set, much of what I could tell you about Bishakha and Shyamal could fit into a small paragraph. This one: At some point in the latter half of the twentieth century, they were arranged to be married. I could also say, though without complete assurance, that they were both from India, but I didn't know where in India they were from. I wasn't sure how old they were. I didn't know how many brothers and sisters they had. I was pretty sure their parents—my grandparents—were all dead. I had no idea what they were like as children or what they hoped their lives would be. I never asked; they never told me.

Don't get me wrong, I'm no Oliver Twist. I grew up with my parents as well as my brother, Sattik, who is nine years older than me. Or, rather, I grew up in the same general time and space continuum as the two people who were responsible for my birth and a sibling who moved out of the house when I was nine. My relationship with my brother has always been warm, in part because the age difference meant he was separated from our family dynamic during my coming of age. But there was a deep void in the relationship with my parents, a pervasive sense of unhappiness that reigned over the home.

My father, an engineer by trade, was mild-mannered and rigid about planning and finances, while also being quite hapless (something I've inherited) and conspicuously distant from my brother and me. My mother, meanwhile, was impulsive (something else I've inherited) and stern. She was the disciplinarian. The personality contrasts were stark: My mother was a social creature who loved gabbing on the phone and taking in pop culture. My father was a nerd who once tried to memorize the periodic table.

But more important than mere personality contrasts was the irreparable schism between them that existed long before I did. It was as if there was an invisible hand that had guided the two least compatible people in the world toward each other. And since the marriage was arranged, my parents couldn't swerve to avoid it. By the time I came along, their distaste for each other was ingrained into the fabric of the household.

The only thing that united them was a genuine pride in being Bengali. It was important to them, but, ironically, it was what I resented most. It was being Bengali that forced these two mismatched souls together, and I looked to escape them at every second. We all tried, in our own way, to make it work, but we were oil, vinegar, and gasoline.

Over time, I learned how to turn my personal trauma into light quips and punchlines. The real stuff, though? That was a little too dark for the Comic Strip.

When I first started exploring comedy seriously, I was working as an assistant producer on an NBC newsmagazine called *Rock Center with Brian Williams,* soon after graduating from Boston University. If you never watched it, don't worry, nobody else did either. It was canceled in less than two years. I was bored there, a young journalist who wasn't given much to do. I also wasn't particularly liked by my higher-ups. If I was to guess, the bosses thought my gregarious personality meant I didn't take my job seriously. Read another way: They found me annoying. I don't blame them. I've spent all day with me, and I don't recommend it.

To make matters worse, I was lonely. My college girlfriend, Michelle, had recently dumped me. She was someone I thought I might marry one day, a woman who was smart and enterprising but, more than anything, showed a degree of selflessness of which many humans aren't capable. I should've realized that she felt differently when she broke up with me over Gchat. If not then, I *definitely* should've taken the hint after the two subsequent breakups, including a final one through an email as she was volunteering at an orphanage in Uganda. It was a brilliant move on her part: She broke up with me in a terrible way and *still* held the moral high ground.

What do sad people do? Some folks see a therapist. Mine was named Jerome, and he was well into his eighties. He had a deep and solemn baritone voice that sounded like James Earl Jones telling a bedtime story. "Soopppaaann. Many people are uncomfortable being alone because theyyyyy were always alone as chillllldren."

Jerome meant well. But during one particularly emotional session when I was pouring out the innards of my soul, admitting that I felt isolated and nervous about not being able to find love, I looked up.

He had fallen asleep.

Come on, man. Jerome had *one job*. The minimum baseline for a therapist is to stay awake while getting paid two hundred dollars an hour. And besides, he was the one with the bedtime voice. I'm the one who should've been sleeping. For five minutes, I sat there confused, wallowing in my inability to date coherently and keep my therapist entertained. I had bombed in front of my own therapist!

Yet I didn't bother finding a new one. I kept seeing Jerome. What does that say about me? (Jerome never could figure it out either.)

You're still awake, right?

Great.

What do other sad people do? Aside from writing Dashboard Confessional songs, some become comedians. Or *try* to become comedians, which is what I did. (I should note here: Plenty of happy people become comedians too.)

I started with an improv class at the Magnet Theater in the Chelsea neighborhood of Manhattan and instantly fell in love with it. Improv is about creating whole new worlds from scratch. Whatever you want. Whenever. And everyone else onstage is forced to go along. *Sir, you'll "yes and" and like it.*

Around that time, I met Manvi Goel, who was also interested in comedy and eventually started improv classes as well. We clicked immediately and became fast friends, talking constantly. We couldn't have been more different, aside from being around the same age. Manvi had been born in India and had grown up there for a while until moving to the suburbs of Washington, D.C. She was technical and academic, where I was impulsive and scatterbrained. She'd attended the Massachusetts Institute of Technology, a school I could get into only with a visitor's pass. Manvi worked as a consultant when we met, a profession I could not have found more unappealing. She was even a Fulbright scholar, which resulted in her spending time conducting research in India. She was Spock; I was Kirk.

Even though we were opposites, she was my best friend. Many of our mutual friends thought we should date, a suggestion we both found ludicrous even though we spent as much time together as a romantic couple would. But we were truly platonic: I thought of her as a sister I could call up any time and make laugh with total non sequiturs for hours. She was also a shoulder to lean on, someone who saw me at my worst and accepted it. We had a running joke that I wouldn't be up to her standards anyway: I went to BU and she only went for Ivy Leaguers.

One time I called her during a particularly tough breakup and said, "Manvi, I just need you to be a friend right now. Don't ask me what happened. Don't ask me to talk about it. I just want to be on the phone and that's it." She didn't say anything. She just sat there on the other end of the line.

We were tempted once, after several glasses of wine in my Harlem apartment, to heed our friends' advice and try to be together. We went to my bedroom and started kissing.

Within seconds, Manvi started cracking up. She started *losing it.* I had never seen her laugh like that before. So I started laughing too. We couldn't take it seriously. Have you ever kissed your sister? Yeah, I didn't want to either. We never tried again. Laughing that hard isn't healthy.

Speaking of unhealthy, after a year or so of improv, I decided to try stand-up. Why share the attention with teammates when you can bask in the glory by yourself? I took a class at the Gotham Comedy Club and started doing open mics. New York City mics, by the way, are brutal. They're terrible ways to test material because the audience is made up of other comedians who don't care about your set. Most aren't paying attention because they're going over their own notes. It was a useful exercise—for a time anyway—because I got used to the feeling of stage discomfort.

In my early attempts to do stand-up, I mostly stuck with observational material, which I found exceedingly difficult. I wasn't good at it. (My first stand-up joke earned a deafening silence: "I'd like to say a few words about race relations. Has anyone here ever had sex while watching NASCAR? No? Then I guess we can't talk about race relations.") I was trying to be

Mitch Hedberg, one of my favorite comedians, or Seinfeld, shoving these wry, witty observations into the lexicon rather than talking about myself. It felt like a parody.

As I started exploring more personal material, I found myself strangely comfortable writing material about being South Asian, despite my thorny relationship with being South Asian. Such went a couple of early jokes:

I've been thinking a lot about the first Indian president. He's always going to be late. Because he's always being "randomly screened" getting onto Air Force One.

The Ebola crisis was the only time in America when a white doctor was considered more dangerous at an airport than a brown person.

One of my favorite jokes came from the *failure* to write a bit. Around Christmas one year, I was at lunch with another comedian friend, Nick. We were trying to write material for a show I had that night. The premise of the joke was "What would happen if Santa Claus was Indian?" I kept coming up with bullshit punchlines: *"Oh! Santa would get stopped by the TSA! Oh! You'd have to leave out chicken tikka masala instead of milk and cookies!"* None of them were any good. After we paid the tab, an older white woman, who appeared to be in her seventies, ambled over to us.

"Excuse me!" she said in a thick Long Island accent. "I couldn't *help* but overhear what you were saying. What if, instead of Santa's workshop, it was a *call center*?"

Then she walked away.

I was about to tell her that this was racist, but how could I? I *loved* the joke. I was trying to find my voice, though at that point I wasn't exactly sure what my voice was. The incongruity of talking about being brown while avoiding my brownness nagged at me. If I talked about it long enough, maybe it would magically fill the holes left by a rocky childhood. I wanted my life to be funny, more comedy than tragedy.

Shortly after I began doing open mics, my father, Shyamal, called me one morning while I was practicing my routine for a show later that night. The phone rang as I silently ran through my set alone in my bedroom, complete with wild gesticulations to an imaginary crowd. At this point, he had been living in India for several years. I didn't know where, mind you, but this was one of his occasional check-in calls that I dreaded. They were short and full of forced chitchat. But this time, I had something more to say than the usual pleasantries about the weather.

"What are you up to, Baba?" my father said. "Baba" is a pet name that Bengali parents often call their children. It also means "father." So, really, we are each other's Baba.

"I'm doing stand-up comedy tonight," I answered.

"What is *stand-up comedy*?" Shyamal steeled himself. He pronounced "stand-up comedy" as if conquering a complicated word for the first time.

"Oh! It's when you stand onstage and tell jokes in front of people," I said.

I knew my father wasn't impressed when I heard him take a deeeeeeeeep sigh. I hadn't thought it was possible to hear a brow furrow.

"Okay. Next topic," Shyamal said, waiting for me to oblige.

I didn't have any other topics, though. Our worlds felt too far apart, and neither of us had ever laid the groundwork to build a bridge between them. *"Okay, next topic"* should've been the tagline to all Deb family conversations, a perpetual ignorance of the questions that were right in front of us. We never tried to understand each other and never examined who we were as people. *Of course* my father didn't ask me why I was doing stand-up. Shyamal and my mother, Bishakha, never knew how much joy I found in making other people laugh, maybe because we were rarely in situations to tell jokes to each other. "Professional comedy" was not even a phrase that made sense in their worlds. But I was just as guilty. In all the check-in calls, I had never even asked him why he had moved to India without telling anybody. I *"next topiced"* that too.

It would be years before Shyamal and I touched the topic of comedy again, even as it became a bigger part of my life. I never discussed it with my mother either, but then again, I never discussed *anything* with her because we had fallen out of touch. We had stopped speaking entirely several years prior to that 2018 set.

When I walked off the stage after that performance, I *did* feel funny. Just not funny in the way you're supposed to feel. In a room full of people who looked like me, where I was supposed to feel comfortable being myself, I felt like an outsider. I had a sneaking suspicion that many of them had a deep bond with their own family and their culture.

Bishakha and Shyamal briefly flashed in my mind, each alone on opposite sides of the globe. Was my father alone in India? Did he have anyone at all? Was my mother even still alive? I was about to enter my thirties and neither parent was a presence in my life. Maybe there was nothing to be done at this point. Maybe it was already too late. But for the first time I didn't want to say, "Okay, next topic."

Soon, I wouldn't have to.

An envelope from Manvi arrived a few weeks later. She had moved out of New York in 2015 or so to work at a startup in Cambridge, Massachusetts, where she met a cute guy named

Jayanth on a dating app. Clearly, making out with *him* didn't crack her up, because they ended up getting engaged.

The elaborate red-and-gold wedding invitation was inscribed:

With the blessings of the all mighty and
Late Smt. Bino Devi and Late Shri Inder Krishna
(Lala Baboo Mal)
Smt. Amita Goel and Shri Anil Goel
request your presence on the occasion of marriage ceremony of
their daughter
Manvi
with
Jayanth

I had known this was coming. Manvi had mentioned to me in the fall that I should save the dates. Normally, it would be "save the date," singular. But this was to be an Indian ceremony, meaning festivities could go on for days and would likely break several fire safety regulations. The wedding was slated for Bengaluru in July, five months after the *Big Brown* show.

When Manvi initially broached the topic, I wasn't sure whether my girlfriend, Wesley, and I would go. It would be expensive. And it was a summer wedding in India.

My god, I thought. *I mean, maybe Manvi and I weren't that close. She moved out of New York a while ago. How many people will really go from the United States? I've never even been to India. Do I even have the vacation time?*

But then another thought came.

Shyamal was in India. I hadn't seen him in eleven years, and by this time he must've been in his midseventies, or older? I didn't want him to pass away before I got to hear his story. I wanted to get to know him, I thought, and it was time for him to get to know me. As if reading my mind, Wesley readily agreed to go. But I still needed to gather the courage to email him and let him know. I finally did, almost a month later.

It said:

> Baba,
> do you by chance live in bangalore? i am planning a trip to india next summer and a friend of mine is getting married there. i will likely have a chance to come see you then.
> Shambo

Shambo is my Indian nickname. Most brown kids have one that their parents gave them. Mine is a reference to the son of the Hindu god Lord Krishna. Shyamal wrote back the next day:

> Hello Shambo Baba
> I am glad to hear from you. I am very glad to know that you are coming to visit Bengaluru in summer. I lived in Bengaluru for some times when I started my first job in September 1967. I still have contact there. Where do you plan to stay there? I shall book the Hotel in advance. Please let me know your schedule in advance. I was not well for some time.
> BABA
> (Shyamal K. Deb)

I didn't know what "not well" meant. I also didn't know that he had ever lived in Bengaluru. Actually, come to think of it, I didn't exactly know where Bengaluru was. But the "not well" line from the email was jarring. I suddenly felt more urgency about the trip. "Not well" holds a different connotation for septuagenarians. I realized that I may have less time than I originally thought.

After a few more rounds of emails in which he insisted

he would meet us anywhere, my father told us that he lived in Kolkata. He added:

> I am already excited to know that I can see you again. Take care.

TWO

"White people have the best lunches."

I told my first joke when I was about six years old. I was in the backseat of a car sitting next to my mother as my father drove us to a family friend's house. A *kaku* was sitting in the front seat. Classic Indian family weekend: get in the car, drive to a relative's house, sit, talk, eat, sit again, talk some more, drive home. I'm generalizing here, but a family weekend for lot of my white friends seemed to involve *doing* things, like hiking, going to the movies, or hanging out at Six Flags. My family just went to suburban sit-on-the-couch-togethers.

These car rides were mostly silent, with a dash of bickering, and though the silence between my parents increased as I got older—the pauses more prolonged, the gaps more awkward—this experience was tolerable enough. We were still at the point in our lives where we could exist in the same physical space together.

My father had a notoriously terrible sense of direction, and, as usual, we had gotten lost. Shyamal could get himself lost driving bumper cars. As we tried to find our way back to the correct road, something came over me: a true gust of inspired comedy.

"You know, Dad could turn a shortcut into a long cut," I blurted out.

My mother cracked up. My first joke. My first open mic. My parents as my first audience. *This was easy.* Even then, I loved the feeling of making someone laugh, especially my mother. She had a deep belly cackle that registered as a five on the Richter scale.

But after that first joke landed, I thought I'd push my luck. I don't know, man. I was six.

"Yeah. AND THEN WE COULD ALL EAT EACH OTHER!" I said.

Bishakha looked at me strangely. Shyamal didn't hear the joke. He was trying to get us wherever we were going only to get us more lost, a metaphor for life if there ever was one. I slunk back in my seat. All right, it was a bomb. What was that line about telling the audience what is funny rather than trying to make them laugh? That *first* chuckle though, so good.

Rick Astley's "Never Gonna Give You Up" was number one on the Billboard charts when I was born in 1988 in Lowell, Massachusetts. I was the original Rick Roll. My birthday is March 15, the Ides of March. The 1980s were weird.

When I was about three, Shyamal moved us to the mean streets of Randolph, New Jersey—the meanest street being the one by the Pathmark where the traffic jams were *brutal.* Until I was about twelve, armed with a middle-class suburban upbringing, I was the model Indian child. There was a vibrant Bengali community in the area, and I became a favorite of all the aunties and uncles—*mashis* and *kakus* in Bengali parlance, typically for close family friends and extended family. (Generally *mama* is for mother's brother, *kaka* is father's brother, *mashi* is mother's sister, *pishi* is brother's sister, *mama*'s wife is *mami*, *kaka*'s wife is *kaki*, and so forth—and all can be applied to family friends.) I spoke Bengali fluently. I took classical Indian vocal lessons and learned how to play the harmonium. At the various annual festivals honoring Hindu deities (known as *pujas*), I performed what I learned in front of those *mashis* and *kakus*. It was what my parents wanted. For a while, I was proud of it too. I *liked* speaking another language and impressing the rest of the Indian community by performing songs they all knew by heart. In turn, my mother enjoyed being able to show me off to her friends.

Our apartment in Randolph was a small two-bedroom, where my mother, brother, and I shared one room, and my father took the other. I shared a bed with my mother, probably far past the age I should have. At the time, I didn't recognize the setup as strange.

Saying my parents had a tumultuous marriage is like looking at a redwood tree and remarking, "Boy, these trunks are elevated." Most of my memories are of the constant fighting. Fighting with each other, with me, with Sattik. At times, it got physical.

There was a coldness that cast a permanent cloud over the house for all of us. This often manifested itself in the mundane. When I came home from school, I felt anxiety, a sense of foreboding, about walking in the door. Not because I was worried about walking into the shouts of fighting parents, but because of the silence. When there wasn't fighting, there was just uncomfortable stillness. We rarely talked about our days. My parents never talked about their past. The future was a nonstarter. One time, when I was about ten, I was playing outside, and I locked myself out of my house on purpose so I had an excuse to go to a family friend's place down the street. It felt safer there. The *mashi* served me dinner. All I really needed was warmth.

Shyamal and Bishakha always *wanted* to provide a safe place, but they didn't know how to do it together. Sometimes their efforts went awry.

In the third grade, while attending Center Grove Elementary School in Randolph, my mother signed me up to be a Boy Scout. As the only brown kid in the troop, I felt like a fish out of curry. At the time, Bishakha had also enrolled me in piano, violin, wrestling, karate, baseball, basketball, soccer, and, in one tragic mishap, advanced figure skating. My schedule was stuffed.

As any Scout knows, the pinewood derby is a big deal. For the uninitiated, the pinewood derby is a Scout event dating back to the 1950s in which the Scout, with the help of his parents, designs a miniature car from a block of wood, which is to be propelled only by gravity. For Shyamal, this was his moment. You see, he was an engineer by trade, and he saw this as a moment to bond with his son. He couldn't teach me how to make a layup on a fast break or torque my hips to properly bash a line drive. But design an aerodynamic car? This was his house, baby.

Shyamal took the block of wood and painstakingly carved it so that it sloped in the front and arced upward in the back. He spoke with poise and authority, traits I rarely saw from him, and explained that carving the wood this way would make the vehicle go downward on the racetrack with more velocity. I was skeptical, not because I didn't believe what he was saying but because I was just generally wary of conversations with him. After the car was sculpted, Shyamal took a can of silver spray paint and gave the block of wood a shiny coat. The car looked amazing. I was proud of it and I was happy that, for once, my father was involved in this creation.

But here's the thing: He is notoriously impatient, another inheritance of mine. He had some sandpapering left to do on the car but didn't want to wait for the paint to dry. So he decided to put it in the microwave. I'm going to say this again: My father—a brilliant, formally trained engineer—put a block of wood with wet paint on it into the microwave so it would dry faster.

As the microwave did its electromagnetic magic, Shyamal and I went into the den to watch television. A few minutes later, one of us—and I don't remember who—noticed that the microwave had been on for a suspiciously long time. By the time we ran into the kitchen to stop it, it was too late. The car was a smoking mess.

Poor, panicked Shyamal went out of his way to convince me that it was fine and that I shouldn't worry. I'm sure he was quietly smoldering as well. His big moment of bonding with his son was ruined.

He was able to salvage the car and repaint it, and we would take it to the big pinewood derby race the next day. I had regained my composure and was ready for the car to do well. After all, I had my engineer dad behind me.

The next step, after designing and burning—*errr,* painting the car—is attaching the axles and wheels. You are supposed to glue the wheels to the axles. Except Shyamal glued the wheels to the car, instead of the axles. This meant the wheels couldn't turn. By the time we realized what he had done, it was time for the races.

I had hope, though. I was a Scout, after all, and according to the Scout handbook, every Scout should be cheerful. We made it to the site of the big event: a local school cafeteria. I took my place at the bottom of a metallic-looking ramp where the cars would cross the finish line, with Shyamal standing nearby. Every few minutes, we'd watch as cars burst forth as if they were shot out of cannons. I saw classmates standing nearby with their fathers, all wearing familiar smiles. My Scout-mandated smile had faded. I was nervous.

Finally, my car was up. I heard the pop. I squinted at my car. It wasn't proceeding like a cannonball. It was barely proceeding at all. It would have lost against the tortoise *and* the hare. It finished in last place. *Okay, not the best start.* Luckily, there were other races. My car would have another shot to advance to the next round. When I took my place at the finish line, my cheerfulness was further dissipating. Another man took my car and placed it at the top of the ramp. *Come on, Car. Let's do this.* Go.

I don't remember how many races my car was in that day. I do vividly remember that in some of them, my car didn't even make it to the end. Either way, it came in last in every single contest. I remember being devastated at the time. But now? I look back on it fondly. It was one of the few warm childhood memories I have with Shyamal.

The rare feelings of warmth gave way to resentment as I observed my friends with their fathers, especially as I became a teenager. For example, I always loved basketball and desperately wanted my dad to help coach me. He didn't really know anything about it, which could explain why I've never been very good. Meanwhile, I would see a lot of my white classmates being taught by their fathers. I'd go over to their houses and hear about their plans to go to a Knicks game. I was jealous. That's how bad it was: I was jealous of people going to see the Knicks play.

In the days of the pinewood derby fiasco, my mother retained the classic helicopter parent gaze. Was there a cap on the number of parent-teacher conferences allowed? She was about to find out! A report card of mostly As? Why aren't they all As? Remember Tiger Mom? My mother was Tiger Mom crossed with Tony the Tiger.

She saw playtime as a distraction. When I turned on the television to watch *Animaniacs, Pinky and the Brain,* or *Hey*

Arnold! after school, she'd cluck disapprovingly. One time she tried to keep me from watching by unplugging the television and saying she didn't know why it wasn't working. I figured the ruse out immediately and plugged it back in. If a disapproving cluck could kill, I might not be alive right now.

For a little while in elementary school, to get me to focus solely on schoolwork, she sat me down to meditate each morning because she thought I was too distracted. It didn't work. All I thought about when my eyes were closed was whether it was actually Pinky, not Brain, who was the smart one. To improve my penmanship, Bishakha would make me do lines. Not the fun kind of lines, mind you, but handwriting. I would spend hours outside of elementary school copying lines out of books I was reading. My penmanship got worse.

My mother and I did spend some quality time together, though, on the days when things were good between us. In elementary school, we'd watch whichever movie came on as part of the *Wonderful World of Disney* feature on ABC. Then came middle school, where we watched—I swear to all the Hindu gods—*7th Heaven* on television. I loved that show. I'd like to think that my mother and I both watched it thinking about the idealized family life we wished we were living. There were the loving and religious parents, Eric and Annie Camden, who instilled strong morals into their perfect children, Matt, Simon, Mary, Ruthie, Lucy, and some cute twins thrown in for good measure. And I must admit that Jessica Biel was one of my first celebrity crushes. The show even had a dog who was named Happy. That's how unsubtle this show was. Many scenes featured the children coming to their mother, Annie, to discuss complicated issues, a concept so strange to me that *Ghostbusters* seemed more realistic.

When I was twelve, we left Randolph and moved to a much larger, four-bedroom home in Howell, New Jersey, which is in the southern part of the state. For reference, it's near Seaside Heights, the beach town where MTV's *Jersey Shore* was filmed. Howell is about 80 percent white, and I was one of the only South Asians in my graduating class of more than four hundred at Howell High School.

At least we had our own bedrooms this time—my mother taking the roomy master and my father claiming a smaller one. Even in middle school, I didn't realize how unusual it was that they slept apart. It was my white friends, especially in high school, who made me aware of it.

One of the times I noticed how different my life was as a brown kid was when my white friend Shaun invited me over for dinner in sixth grade. It was my first year in Howell, and he lived a short walk away. We played Wiffle ball outside with some other neighborhood kids, and then Wendy (Shaun's mom) made us tacos. We sat around the dinner table, along with Dylan (Shaun's brother) and Patrick (Shaun's father). They each took turns telling everybody about their day after dinner was served. Sitting together for dinner wasn't an obligation for this family. It was enjoyable.

All I could think was, *What the fuck is this?*

In retrospect, I see this dichotomy for what it was: happy versus unhappy. Back then, it was brown and white.

Bishakha made food for us, morning and evening. She would leave cereal out for me in the morning and, occasionally, a banana. But I refused to eat the bananas, so she eventually gave up. (She won in the end, though, because I now have a banana for breakfast every day.)

In the evenings, we ate Bengali food—she was an excellent chef, and Sundays were her days to cook. Her specialty was a fish mustard curry. The odor of masala would waft through the air like a wayward hot air balloon. I miss that smell, actually.

Some of her culinary efforts were a bit off. In kindergarten, my mother sent me to school every day with a piece of cheese. Not gummy bears or animal crackers or the other cool snacks my classmates had. I had a giant lunchbox with a piece of cheese and a juicebox. Every single day, I'd open up my lunchbox hoping for something different. It was cheese. Every fucking day. *White people have the best lunches.*

There were times the three of us would eat together (or the four of us, before Sattik left for college), but it was rare. And those dinners were quick and silent. I didn't think much about why we ate separately. I processed it very simply as, *I would rather eat while watching television than sit here in silence with my family.* It didn't strike me as strange until I became friends with kids like Shaun.

When I went over to Shaun's house, I bonded with Wendy. Shaun's mother was always kind and approachable. She always insisted on being called Wendy, which I found strange. No Indian *mashi* or *kaku* would *ever* accept that. I knew that Shaun talked about girls with his mother because he told me. In one of our early visits, Wendy pulled me aside and said she was worried that Shaun wasn't making friends in school. She punctuated this thought by saying, "I want Shaun to GO OUT and then MAKE OUT!" I was so jealous of Shaun. What a mom. I wanted to both make out and have a mother who wanted me to make out.

The year I met Shaun was also the year I first told my mother about a crush. A classmate of mine at Howell Township Middle School South—we'll call her Phoebe—had a friend tell me that she "like likes" me. It was the first time in my life this had happened. Phoebe had big curly hair and a sweet personality. That she had a friend tell me directly about her feelings was very mature, given that my generation was partial to romantic feelings expressed anonymously through AOL Instant Messenger profiles.

I was enamored by Phoebe's affection, but I had no idea what to do.

So, naturally, emboldened by Wendy's pep talk about going out and making out, I went home and asked my mother what she thought about Phoebe "like liking" me. Bishakha put her book down, stared, and said nothing for a moment. And then she just *laughed and laughed,* as if I were Chris Rock at the Apollo. Then she walked out of the room. We didn't approach the topic of girls for at least another decade.

When I had my disastrous first kiss in eighth grade (involving braces and a big *clink!*), I never told her. I wanted to, but I didn't know if my mother had ever gone on a date. That excitement and anticipation you feel about someone new was probably as foreign to her as being arranged was to me. The topic felt like it was off-limits in a way it wasn't for any of my white friends whose parents had all been through the adolescent misery that eventually culminates in "love marriages," as my father would call them. Many of my white classmates had parents who understood heartbreak stemming from bad dating experiences, or the high that comes from a crush giving you the faintest bit of attention. The generation that had grown up in America before us had gone out and then made out.

More important, I couldn't talk to Bishakha about the alienation I felt at school as one of the only children of color, or how I was having trouble making friends. She wanted me to be focused on academics and that was nonnegotiable. When she felt my grades weren't high enough, she would snatch the activities that meant the most to me, like flag duty or an elementary school basketball team, without offering an opportunity for protest. She may have thought she was motivating me, but my response to the resulting social alienation was an attempt to suppress my brownness in the hope of finding friends.

I wanted to fit in, and I viewed my parents' insistence on academic perfection as a by-product of our brown culture. It's a stereotype of Asian parents, but it was an accurate one in our household. Their relentless focus on report cards seemed designed to torture me. I never thought much about what their childhoods had been like, what lessons their lives had taught them, or how those lessons shaped them as parents. My reaction was classically juvenile. Instead of heeding their advice, I became a wannabe class clown. In eighth grade, the same year as my first kiss, I submitted an entire short story with such character names as Seymour Butts, Ben Dover, and Mike Rotch, which got me kicked out of the end-of-the-year celebration. I was acting out, period. I skipped homework assignments, and when teachers sent "homework slips" home to inform Shyamal and Bishakha that I wasn't keeping up, I intercepted them and forged my mother's signature. I was committing fraud as a child.

Toward the end of middle school, the anger I felt became the only constant in my life. I completely rejected the brown side of myself. Calling it a *side* seems unfair. Your culture isn't a *side*. Boxes have sides. But culture and heritage? It's who you are. Still, I refused to believe I was Indian. *I'm different,* I told myself, *I have to be different than this.* The situation at home became more unbearable as I navigated my teenage years. My parents were fighting more, and my mother's disposition swung rapidly and unpredictably from calm to choppy waters. I distinctly remember money being a sticking point, although I never figured out specifically why. Bishakha took a job as a cashier at Drug Fair, a local pharmacy, where she made about sixteen thousand dollars a year. I suspected at the time that she took the job to get herself out of the house and because she wanted to have some financial independence from my father. I blamed arranged marriage, Hinduism, and India for the ills of the household, even though I didn't know enough about any of those things. I just knew I wanted distance from whatever culture had forced my parents together and produced this misery. I stopped playing the harmonium and performing at Indian festivals. When my parents hosted Bengali family gatherings, I started avoiding the party because I was embarrassed by the number of saris and dhotis being worn around my home. I became a self-loathing Bengali child.

I grew to idealize whiteness, which I conflated with safety and easy communication. This desire to be white didn't come from feeling socially or politically marginalized because of my skin color. It was about white suburban moms who made after-school snacks and asked my friends about the girls they liked and the teachers they hated. The sex talk with Indian parents is the same talk as the one about what college you should go to: Get good grades and you don't have to worry about either.

At the end of middle school, my parents' scant tolerance of each other shifted to intolerance. They separated sometime around 2001. When I was in high school, they officially, mercifully, divorced.

I was relieved. Divorce isn't uncommon in the United States. But it *is* uncommon among arranged marriages, especially in India. By design, arranged marriages are transactional in nature. The love, in theory, comes later. Perhaps this is why, in the United States, the divorce rate among Indian-Americans is estimated among experts to be between 1 and 15 percent, according to the *Washington Post*. It's hard to pinpoint a precise number for this, and the United States government doesn't track Indian-American divorces. But the national average is closer to 50 percent (although this number varies among age groups).

After the divorce, my relationship with each parent improved, though it was a low bar to clear. Shyamal moved to a small apartment about thirty minutes away from Howell, and it was decided that I would stay with my mother. I didn't object, more due to a sense of inertia than a desire to pick one parent over the other. Every time my father called and I saw his name on the caller ID, I cringed. The scars were still there. We had become acquaintances by that time, nothing more. The conversations with my father would last no more than a few minutes and consist of small talk. *How's the weather? What did you eat today? Click.* We'd occasionally meet up for dinner and hear only the sound of our chewing.

I also changed in high school after my parents separated, physically and mentally. I became as independent as one can get as a fifteen-year-old. As a symbol of my newfound self-rule, I grew an afro and started wearing tie-dye to class. This was, I think, when I shifted my parents to peripheral characters in my life. I didn't need Bishakha's instruction as to what extracurricular clubs I should join, and she didn't give it. By then she realized I wanted to be left alone. And she obliged. I got a job as a cashier at a grocery store and saved up money to buy my own car. Plus she was working her Drug Fair job full-time and wasn't getting home until the evenings anyway, so I came and went as I pleased.

I applied to colleges on my own: New York University, Rutgers University, Boston University, Boston College, and Berklee College of Music. I had played classical piano my whole life and briefly entertained making my living in music. Although I was living with my mother, Bishakha didn't know what colleges I applied to until acceptance letters started coming in. Thankfully, BU gave me a big scholarship, so I made the decision to go there.

I didn't cringe when my mother called me during college, which was the best our relationship ever was. When I came home on winter breaks, we occasionally watched television together. You couldn't quite call us close, but the relationship was comfortable.

She never visited me at BU, but I visited her at home. At least then we were in touch.

But something shifted after college. I got my first job working at the *Boston Globe*, before moving to New York to work at NBC. I started to notice that calls with Bishakha were becoming less frequent, and I knew that her contact with my brother, Sattik, was rare or nonexistent. When we did talk, she sounded sadder than usual. I didn't know why and didn't summon the emotional wherewithal to find out.

Days without us talking became weeks. Weeks became months. Months became years. And as I turned thirty, I realized that my mother and I had ceased all substantive contact for at least three years, if not more.

After receiving the wedding invitation from Manvi in 2018, I made the decision to go to India and see Shyamal. But I didn't feel it would be right to fly around the world to reconnect with him and not put in some of the same effort with Bishakha. At the very least, I knew I needed to see where she was. I was more nervous about this connection than the one with my father and bracing myself for how she might react to the outreach. I felt guiltier about having let this relationship deteriorate in the way that it had, knowing that my mother was just across the Hudson River. There were several days when I wanted to pick up the phone and call her, but I couldn't bring myself to do it.

As we approached Mother's Day that year, months after that *Big Brown* set, I decided I was ready.

For most people, Mother's Day is a time to pay tribute to the women who suffered through pregnancy to birth and then raise them. The woman who cleaned up after them, supported them financially, cooked for them, talked them through the bullies in middle school, excitedly sent them to prom, and, tearfully, sent them to college. But for me during any other year, this would be just another Sunday.

On the few days Bishakha's face appeared in my mind, I swam in an ocean of self-reproach. I felt bad for not being there for her, even as I tried to convince myself that she and my father were mere footprints on a path I had long ago left behind. She was a woman in her seventies—it was a guess, I wasn't certain of her age—who was brought up in another country, had little understanding of technology, and who lived by herself in a New Jersey suburb with no family to look after her. She had no one to lift boxes for her. She had no one to install a light bulb or fix her wireless Internet. If she fell, neither of her two sons would be by her side to help her, since she had fallen out with each of them. She was also no longer in contact with Atish, her brother in Toronto, and was very much alone.

It's painful to face the fact that your own mother is alive, less than a two-hour drive away, and you have no idea what she does on a daily basis. This was assuming she even still lived in New Jersey. It's easier not to think about the guilt when you don't think at all.

Call, I demanded myself. *Call her now.*

Of course, there was one problem: I didn't have her number. I had a cell phone number for her, but she didn't use it. I knew that because I had purchased the phone for her in college and I had paid the bill on it for several years as part of a family plan. I noticed the usage on her phone was mostly zero. I called it anyway. It kept ringing. Was this cell phone even in her possession anymore?

Sitting in my living room, I briefly wondered if there was no way to get in touch with her. I called another number: my childhood home phone number, with a somewhat ridiculous expectation that it still belonged to my mother. It didn't.

Luckily, buried in an email from 2014, I found another number. I dialed. After three rings, I heard my mother's voice. I leaned forward on my couch and gripped the phone tightly. I could feel my blood pulsing.

"Hello?" my mother said.

"Ma, it's Shambo," I said, trying to project a sense of calm that didn't exist.

"Oh. How are you?" my mother said. I could hear that she too was displaying that same faux sense of calm. She sounded old and tired, as if a lifetime of loss and loneliness had taken its toll. I, perhaps recognizing this, summoned my childhood Bengali in an attempt to alleviate the awkward space in which we found ourselves.

"I am doing well. How are you doing?" I nudged.

"I am doing well. What's new? How's work?" *My mother.* It was terrible, uncomfortable small talk.

"Work is very busy. I write a lot about theater, film, and television. What else do I write about? A lot of comedy," I answered. This was during my time writing for the culture section, before switching to the NBA beat.

"Really? I saw you on MSNBC," my mother said. Her voice became lighter. She was recalling a recent segment during which I was discussing whether Oprah would run for president in 2020. Meanwhile, my organs felt like they were splitting. The only time my mother had seen my face in the last few years was in a cable television news hit.

"I see a lot of Broadway shows now. It's a good break for me from politics. When you cover politics, you don't sleep at all. You're always working and checking your email. Now I don't work very much on weekends," I said.

My mother asked me if I was still living in my apartment

in Harlem. I had lived in Harlem for about five years, and my mother had never seen either of the two apartments I lived in while there. I told her yes, but this wasn't true. I had moved in with my girlfriend, Wesley, something I didn't, at this point, feel was necessary to tell my mother. She suggested I buy a house.

I quietly sighed. She didn't quite understand the New York City real estate market.

"I don't have that kind of money," I gently chided her. "If you want to buy anything in New York, you have to put down a minimum fifty thousand dollar down payment."

She suggested I go outside of New York. I told her I'd see. She asked me if I'd be going on MSNBC again. I said maybe, but that I didn't discuss politics on the air anymore since I wasn't covering it.

"The next time you're on, why don't you let me know?" my mother said.

My stomach had unclenched slightly. We had advanced from Peak Awkwardness to Genuine Catch-Up. Impulsively, I stammered a sentence that seemed inconceivable a few minutes before.

"If in the next month—if you're not—if . . ." I paused to gather myself. "Do you want to come to New York to watch a Broadway show sometime?"

Silence.

"Uh, the last time I saw a Broadway show? When was that?" My mother had misunderstood the question, possibly because of my stammering.

I clarified: "No, I'm saying if there is a Broadway show you want to see, you can come to New York if you want. I can get tickets."

Another pause, this one less prolonged.

"If we can go, let me know," she said. "Weekday or weekend?"

"Whenever is convenient for you."

Pause. I could hear her breathe.

"Yes, let me know."

"There are lots of good shows out there. There's a new show you might like—"

"I've heard you're doing comedy now." My mother changed the subject, not wanting to test our good fortune.

"Yes, I've done a lot of comedy. I try to do one or two shows every month," I responded, without a clue as to how she had found out.

My mother asked me if I was getting married. That, of course, would be news about which she could get excited. I laughed and told her about Wesley. That she had graduated from Harvard Law School and was a practicing lawyer. I took immense pride in telling her that.

I said that we could come over soon and that she could meet Wesley if she wanted.

Another pause.

"I have nothing. If you want to come, that would be great news."

When my mother said she had nothing, she didn't just mean her calendar was empty. I knew what she meant.

"This would be glorious news to meet your girlfriend," she added. I could hardly believe what I was hearing. She would never have said that in college. In fact, she didn't.

"Okay, we can rent a car and come see you."

We said our goodbyes and hung up the phone. I sighed deeply. Have you ever walked into an ocean that's just a little too cold? It's a deeply uncomfortable shock to the senses at first, but you hope your body gets used to it as you submerge yourself farther into the water. And then you take another step. And then another.

I was one step in and ankle deep.

THREE

"I almost did not recognize you."

It was hot. I mean, really hot. It took approximately eight seconds after I stepped outside to reconsider the wisdom of this trip, though I shouldn't have been surprised. After all, we were in Kolkata in July.

For those of you who might need a reference point: Take a blazing ball of fire and put it in a microwave, and you have Kolkata in July. Add in a sprinkle of monsoon season and you have a recipe for unbearable discomfort.

Wesley and I stepped outside the Netaji Subhash Chandra Bose International Airport after a four-hour flight from Dubai (which was preceded by a fifteen-hour flight from New York). We emerged to the chaotic pulse of the city. The honks of cabs. Yells in Bengali. Police officers ordering cars to keep moving. It was worse than Times Square at the height of tourist season.

I felt overwhelmed, but Wesley looked strangely calm about everything. Knowing her, that made sense.

We met shortly after I started working at the *Times* in early 2017. For a brief period, the reporters for the culture section were being cycled through the breaking news desk, also called the Express desk. It was an ambitious section, known for producing the paper's best digital content. Rotating culture reporters through the section was an effort to get us to move faster and be more like the reporters there.

During my first week on Express, I was assigned to write about a story that had gone viral. A gate agent for United Airlines refused to allow two teenagers to board a flight to Minneapolis from Denver because they were wearing leggings, incurring the wrath of the Internet. It turned out that the teenagers were flying with "pass riders," tickets given to friends and family of airline employees. United claimed that passengers had to meet a certain dress code to use these tickets, so I posted a message on Twitter asking the public to write or call with their stories of flying with pass riders. Many did. (That includes one person who was working at a temp agency answering phones. He reached out again more than a year later after starting as a writer for Stephen Colbert, and we've since become friends.) I wrote the story and it went online. Easy peasy.

After it published, I got a message from someone named Wesley Dietrich, offering a friend who could talk to me for the story.

I thought this was a little odd, considering that my story was already up. I thanked her for the offer but didn't think much of it. We started exchanging messages. I learned that Wesley was finishing up law school and also concluding a gig working for Al Franken, who at the time was a Democratic senator from Minnesota. It also turned out we had a mutual friend who had covered the 2016 presidential campaign with me. I let her know that I'd love to get drinks if she was ever in New York, though I never expected to hear from her again.

A couple of weeks later, she followed up to say that she was in town and that she'd like to get a drink. We went to a bar next door to the Magnet Theater, where I had taken improv classes years before and still occasionally performed. I was blown away by her. She was barely over five feet tall, with striking blue eyes, blonde hair, and a face that reminded me a bit of Reese Witherspoon. She was beautiful, like way out of my league. In my head, all I could think was: *Play the* New York Times *card early and often. She won't know how junior you are. Or just make something up. Either way, you need a plan.*

I spoke too fast and perhaps a bit too loudly on that first date, much like during my first ever stand-up routine. I was nervous and wanted to impress her. Wesley, an Arkansas native, was confident, smart, and quick-witted. Sometimes, especially when discussing politics, she would get animated and gesture wildly.

When the bartender asked us if we wanted any food, I flubbed. I answered on behalf of Wesley and said, "No, we're good." As I learned later, she *had* wanted snacks. I could've gone for some fries too, but I wanted to give her an out just in case she wasn't having a good time. Besides, who orders food on a first date in 2017?

Like me, she came from divorced parents. Except she was the product of a second marriage for each of her parents, who each remarried again after that. This was a real-life Brady Bunch situation. When we first met, Wesley joked that she was the Tiffany Trump of her family (in chronology only).

Before our second date, which featured cookies from Levain (a bakery on the Upper West Side with cookies as large as my head) and a bottle of wine in Central Park followed by an improv show at the Magnet, I told a friend that I was in love and that I was going to marry this girl. I was being facetious, but not by much.

When we first started dating, Wesley was a bit cold, or so I thought. She had this terribly annoying habit of going to sleep in the middle of a conversation when she was living in Massachusetts and I was in New York.

Our texts, early on, would go something like this:

ME: How was your evening?

WESLEY: It was fine, just had a lot of work to do.

ME: That's great! Did you get it done?

WESLEY: Yeah, but . . .

ME: But . . . ?

ME: Hello?

ME: Are you there?

ME: Are you kidding me?

She came back to visit New York a few weeks before her commencement. We stopped at a bar near my apartment for a nightcap, and I popped the question: Can I come to your graduation? Wesley looked at me as if I were the Boston Strangler. Let me rephrase: She looked at me as if I were popping *the* question. She said no, after a long and awkward pause, giving me the impression that our relationship was doomed. *I really should've ordered some snacks for the table.*

But we kept seeing each other, and very quickly, she became my biggest advocate—for my career, my comedy, and my investigation into my family history.

Shortly before we took off from New York, Wesley and I sat in an Irish pub at JFK, munching on mediocre chicken fingers. She ordered two glasses of champagne for us and asked me how I was feeling.

"Like I want to get there. I know that's not a very good answer," I replied.

"No deeper thoughts or observations?" Wesley pressed.

"I have been trying to figure out how I feel all day, or probably for a couple of months, and I haven't figured it out yet." I was curt. "I don't think the reality has hit me yet that I'm about to see my dad."

"Maybe you'll find out when we get there," Wesley offered.

"Maybe I'll find out when we get there," I repeated robotically.

On the plane, we were both anxious; neither of us had any idea what lay ahead. But despite my anxiety, I did learn during the plane ride that Oscar from *The Office* has a small part in 2003's *The Italian Job.* I mention this because it's precisely the kind of fact you only have the pleasure of discovering on a long flight since there is no other scenario in which you would willingly watch *The Italian Job.*

Outside the airport, I craned my neck, looking for Shyamal, but found only a cacophony of greeters, honks, and yelling in Bengali.

"Ekhene cab ache!"

"Thumi kothai jethe chau?"

"Thomar bag knie sadjho kor bo?"

It was a disorderly symphony, the kind of stuff Tchaikovsky was *not* made of. I was weighed down by an assortment of bags and plane pillows, and the sweat beads had already begun dripping from my brow. I looked around, pacing back and forth, trying to appear calm. But the noises outside were nothing compared to the frantic questions in my head. My eyes searched the crowd for a frail old man in his mid- to late-seventies. Maybe he'd have a walker. A wheelchair? *A new wife?* I turned to Wesley and said, "I have no idea what kind of life I'm about to walk into."

It was the worst kind of semi-blind date. You know, one with your father, whom you hadn't seen in more than eleven years and knew virtually nothing about.

I pulled out my cell phone and dialed the contact that said

DAD. That's a weird way of describing a father, right? "A contact that said DAD?" But it was indicative of our relationship at that moment. I knew that he existed, but he was just a phone contact, in the same way that DAN FROM THE NETWORKING EVENT YOU HATED lingered in your contact list: something between a stranger and a forgotten childhood acquaintance.

In 2007, my freshman year of college, Shyamal came to visit me in Boston at the beginning of my spring semester. I don't remember much of the visit, other than that he bought me lunch at my favorite Thai restaurant on campus, Noodle Street, before taking me to a local grocery store for some supplies. I didn't realize at the time that this would be the last time I would see him for eleven years. I might have given him a better goodbye if I had.

The next month, I noticed that I hadn't heard from him for at least a couple of weeks. My father used to call every Sunday like clockwork. So I called him. Usually, if my father saw a missed call from me, he would immediately call me back. But he didn't. So I called again and left a voicemail. If my father saw two missed calls and a voicemail from me, he would fly to Boston to make sure I was okay. It's true that we weren't close, but he desperately wanted to be, and as I grew older he tried, in his own awkward way, to bond with me.

Shyamal still didn't call me back. At this point, I was worried. He was an older man living by himself as an immigrant in a country that hadn't worked out for him. Spring break was coming up, and I decided that I would knock on his door when I got home.

Right before the break, I get an email from him. He told me that he was sick and that he was no longer in New Jersey. I immediately responded: "Where are you? Are you in a hospital in

New York? I'll come visit you."

I was startled by his response:

"I'm in India."

Shyamal didn't know when he'd be back. I had never even been to India. He said he was too ill to live in New Jersey on his own and that he had left for medical treatment.

He never came back.

Throughout the next decade, I never found out where, exactly, he was living. Isn't that bizarre? My father moved to another country without telling anybody, and I wasn't fazed. It was one step from a parental ghosting. I would've asked more questions after a mediocre online dating attempt.

Perhaps my reticence was born of the same guilt I felt about the situation with my mother. I've always had this nagging feeling that I didn't do right by Shyamal, that I wasn't a good enough son to him and didn't give us a chance to work on our relationship. I didn't want to know why he was too sick to stay in the country because I was sure I partially caused it. I always had this thought in the back of my head that *maybe,* if I had taken the time to engage with him in a meaningful way, instead of looking at myself as the aggrieved child of immigrant parents who didn't *get* him, he would have felt comfortable communicating about his need to leave. Knowing less about my father's situation allowed me to remain blissfully ignorant of the role I played in his decision to do so.

As the years passed, and my father would call from India, our conversations grew more irregular. He'd never learn anything about me and I'd never learn anything about him. The calls just let me know that he was still alive. Sometimes he'd ask if we could video chat. I always found some reason not to. Seeing his face would make it too real.

Outside baggage claim in Kolkata, the time to avoid seeing his face was quickly running out. Days before, he had emailed us a picture of himself since he knew I might not remember what he looked like. Of course, the picture he sent featured him wearing sunglasses, a Bart Simpson T-shirt with cut-off sleeves, and a baseball cap, which is the exact picture you send someone when you *don't* want to be recognized.

I called my father. "Yeah, we're on the sidewalk," I said.

I turned to Wesley and put on a brave face: "It's not that hot here. Not right now, anyway."

"I think he was waiting—" I said, and suddenly stopped in my tracks. Wesley spotted a man striding confidently out the arrival doors on a mission, like the brown Kool-Aid Man.

"Oh my god, I think that's him," I said.

It was an unexpected, remarkable sight. When I last saw him at Noodle Street, I remember thinking how unhealthy he looked. Now, in India eleven years later, he looked tanned, rested, and spirited—with almost as much hair as I have. He wore a white dress shirt with black pants, and he sported a fresh haircut. That he still had hair to cut was a surprise to me—one of many, I'd find out. His muscles had tone. He didn't have a Dad-Bod. It was just a . . . Bod. He had the kind of glowing, confident tan of someone who had strolled onto a golf course smoking a Cohiba and blasted an 80 blindfolded. He was earnest and genuinely excited.

"Welcome to India!" he said to both of us. "Said" is an understatement. It was more like a roar. Everything out of his mouth was a yell.

"WELCOME TO INDIA!"

He joyfully handed Wesley a dozen or so miniature roses, their stems carefully wrapped in aluminum foil to keep them fresh. I got a pat on the head.

"WOW, YOU'RE A GROWN-UP MAN NOW! I ALMOST DID NOT RECOGNIZE YOU."

"It's been many years, Dad."

"I WAS WAITING THERE WATCHING EVERY DOOR. HOW COULD YOU COME OUT? I'M WAITING THERE LIKE A SECURITY GUARD. A COUPLE OF TAILORS ARE HERE. ONE FOR YOU, ONE FOR HER."

"You know we're not the ones getting married, right?" I answered.

"I DON'T KNOW ANYTHING ABOUT YOU! COME ON."

FOUR

"My son is a star!"

Wesley and I piled our bags into the trunk of the car and climbed into the backseat, while Shyamal occupied the front. And it began: our first car ride in India, which was really great training for a zero-gravity spacewalk should life ever come to that. There are no driving rules in India, at least none that I could see. Our driver routinely swerved and cut off cars or was on the receiving end of similar chaos. In New Jersey, this could get you killed. In Kolkata, which is located in the eastern part of the country near the border with Bangladesh, it was just a Wednesday.

Every few seconds, the driver honked. It wasn't out of road rage. All the other drivers honked too. It was a way of self-policing on the road. Honk or get bonked. We tried to converse in the car, which was an exercise in futility.

"MY [HONK] TENNIS COURT IS [HONK] JUST BESIDE YOUR [HONK] HOTEL!" my dad yelled.

"You still [HONK] play tennis?"

"OF COURSE! [HONK] TODAY, I PLAYED. MONDAY, WEDNESDAY, AND FRIDAY. [HONK] PLUS GOLF TWICE A MONTH."

Cutting through all the Kolkata noise, I was relieved to hear he wasn't the slowly dying man I knew all those years ago, much to my surprise. And as I found out during the cab ride, he had other interests too. Constant activity doesn't leave time for the mind to wander.

The conversation turned to Wesley, who, upon interrogation, told my father she had recently graduated from law school at Harvard. Shyamal lowered his voice a bit.

"Very good! Very good! I am very proud of you. I have taken two courses at MIT and Harvard."

"Really?" I cut in.

"Of course! Have you not seen my résumé?"

"You know, I have not seen your résumé. Not recently."

"My dad was a very good lawyer. Your grandfather. A famous criminal lawyer. He never lost a case."

We were twenty minutes into the ride. It was the most substantive conversation my father and I had ever shared. In that moment, it hit me that I had never really thought about my grandparents before.

Then came this exchange:

"Sopan, could you recognize me? Have I changed a lot?"

"I did recognize you, but it was much different than I expected."

"What did you expect?"

"I don't know. You seem like you're living your best life right now."

"REALLY?! MY HEART HAS BEEN VIBRATING FOR THE LAST FOUR MONTHS. HOW CAN I SEE MY LONG-LOST SON?"

"Honestly, I don't know what I was expecting. I'm happy to see you're so active," I said.

"You look much different than when I last saw you." He paused for a split second. "You've put on weight."

"Thank you."

My father and I were dipping our toes in. We circled each other, a bit cautiously at first, like professional wrestlers before they lock horns. The last time we had an in-person conversation, I was adjusting to life as a freshman in college and being on my own for the first time. Aside from doing well in class, I was singularly focused on fitting in on campus, a daunting task for someone who had always felt like an outsider. I was unsure of myself. I cared a lot about what other people thought. In high school, people my age were still wearing those puka shell surfer necklaces that seemed really stylish. I was so thirsty for acceptance that I'd ask other students if I could wear theirs for a couple of hours just so people thought I had my own. It never occurred to me to just buy one. College was my chance to walk into frat parties and seem *cool*. I was in the midst of a search for the biggest, coolest friend group in Massachusetts.

More than a decade later, I was more mature and centered, comfortable with my path in life. The version of myself that Shyamal was seeing had room for him that wasn't there when I was eighteen.

"HOW DID YOU LIKE DUBAI?" my dad asked—no, yelled—about the city in which we'd had a one-night layover the night before.

"Dubai was wonderful," I answered.

"Yes, Dubai is one of the leading developing cities in the world. Lot of wealth is over there," he said.

"Have you been there recently?" I asked.

"Not recently. A long time back."

Small talk about geopolitics—very good, I thought. Wesley told him we were more excited about India than Dubai, to which my father responded with a hearty laugh.

I should take a second and describe that laugh. I have a terrible chuckle that often runs on a two-second delay. It's the kind that embarrasses friends at parties, which probably helps explain why I was rarely invited to any in college.

But my father's? Imagine Santa Claus yelling, "HO, HO, HO!" but in a high-pitched staccato and through a loudspeaker. When Shyamal finds something funny, it's best to board up surrounding windows. It's actually not too dissimilar from Bishakha's laugh, just in a higher register.

"We shall show you India very well. Did you have a little bit of studies about India? The Mughals and all that?" Shyamal asked, foreshadowing an amusing motif of our Indian education.

"A little bit. Honestly, we wanted to learn as much as we could on this trip."

We were both getting a bit more comfortable. My heart was beating at a more normal pace, and I let my shoulders hunch a bit. Shyamal lowered his voice.

"How about music? Are you practicing music at all?"

He remembered. My parents, against my wishes, had made me take classical piano lessons starting when I was six. I hated it. I hated practicing Beethoven. I hated how exact you had to be. If Mozart wanted something quick in this section (sorry, "allegro"), it had to be quick. You didn't color outside the lines. Eventually, after about eight years, I stopped going to lessons and started picking up jazz on my own. I loved the concept of improvisation.

I was one of the better piano players for my age until high school, but I didn't practice enough and never improved. Even though I auditioned for the Berklee College of Music, I was never skilled enough to do it full-time. I was, however, good enough to be in several cover bands throughout my life, including one called the Streetlight Band. When my mother and father took me to my lessons, I doubt they envisioned my abilities peaking with a cover of Bryan Adams's "Summer of 69" at Edgar's Pub on the Jersey Shore.

Shyamal was a musician himself, as he reminded me. An accordion player. He was a less cool version of Weird Al. I have flashes of memories from him playing when I was a child, but it was the same three songs over and over again. One of them was "Edelweiss," from *The Sound of Music.*

Back to the roar.

"I'VE GOT A VERY BEAUTIFUL PIANO FOR YOU," Shyamal said at a busy intersection. "I'VE BEEN PLAYING IT FOR THE LAST EIGHT YEARS. I GOT IT TUNED! THE TUNING CHANGES EVERY THREE OR FOUR MONTHS BECAUSE OF THE CHANGE OF CLIMATE, BUT MY PIANO IS IN VERY GOOD SHAPE. I'VE BEEN WAITING HOURS FOR YOU TO COME AND PLAY. I'LL TAKE PICTURES."

In my mind, I quickly ran through the visuals of my father videotaping me at this highly anticipated piano summit, in which I'm yelling, "I got my first real six-string. Bought it at the five-and-dime!" or some other bar-band classic.

The driver lurched back and forth with no warning, the high-pitched car honks complemented by Shyamal's energetic squeals. I've never done cocaine, but boy, did it feel like it might've been the boost I needed to keep up.

"This is Kolkataaaaa. Did you know six people got the Nobel Prize from this city?" he said. My father has a verbal tic, which was exhibited many times throughout the trip. When he wanted to teach us something, he would elongate the word or subject he was trying to teach us about. So Kolkata became Kolkataaaa. Mughals became Mughaaaaals. Shyamal rambled on about the writings of Rabindranath Tagore, the legendary poet, essayist, and writer, who won the Nobel Prize in Literature in 1913, the first Asian to do so.

Tagore's work was formative during my father's childhood, or so he said. Beverly Cleary was during mine, but I didn't feel like explaining Ramona Quimby to him.

"Wesley and I are both excited about the food," I told Shyamal. We were. I never rejected this side of my brownness. I have always loved Indian food, as does Wesley.

"My plan is to give you all home-cooked foods. My cook is very good. Yesterday, I bought special fresh fish for you. Various types of fishes. You cannot get this fish in America. Brand-new good fish. We'll take care of you. I've got Indian white wine, red wine, and Indian beer," Shyamal said. I had never had a drink with him before.

"Now we're talking," I answered. It surprised me to learn that he had his own cook, though we soon realized that this is very common in India. When we were initially hammering out the details of the trip, Shyamal asked us to bring a gift for a woman who stayed with him. I had quietly wondered if he had remarried without mentioning it. He hadn't. It turned out that Shyamal was referring to his cook, Suparna.

Part of the reason I resented my father when I was young was that I didn't feel like I had one. There was a cultural gap between us—his upbringing in India never yielded to American assimilation—as well as a generational one: Shyamal is almost fifty years older than me.

In high school, I had a friend named Paul who lived down the street. His father, Stan, played the guitar and taught Paul, who is my age, how to play. They were in a classic rock band together, which performed covers of the Beatles, Billy Joel, and Fleetwood

Mac—music that I loved. In high school, Stan invited me to be part of the band as the new keyboardist. This was the Streetlight Band. I felt more of a connection to Stan than I did to my own dad. There was no way I could talk to Shyamal about how *Rumours* was one of the best albums ever made. He didn't know what *Rumours*, Fleetwood Mac, or actual rumors were.

What fatherhood meant in his mind and my desire for what I believed to be the quintessential American experience my white friends had were two vastly different things. To Shyamal, being a father was a black-and-white equation about putting forth the hard work through whatever means necessary so that the family could *survive*. In America, in theory, it should have been easier to do that. That's why he immigrated here.

I never saw it that way. As a kid in a New Jersey suburb, life wasn't just about survival. It was a kind of privilege I never realized I had. I wanted our relationship to be about playing catch or riding bikes together. I wanted Shyamal to know my friends and teach me how to shave. I wanted someone to talk to about girls and tell me where babies came from. That was America, I thought, especially considering the experience my white childhood friends were having. Where I wanted less from my mother in many ways—less pressure, less interference—I badly wanted more from Shyamal.

The cultural gap was widened further by my father's pride in being an immigrant. I saw his pride as a burden, especially in middle school and high school, where feeling like an outsider was a constant. Hardly anyone in class looked like me. If they did, I bet I would have spent time with other parents similar to Shyamal, and my assumptions about race and parenting would have been different. These feelings, specifically the ones I had equating whiteness with being American, weren't justified or rational. With the benefit of time, I can say they were wrong.

The truth is that I'm not sure that my relationship with Shyamal ever had a chance. Even if my parents had had a stable, healthy marriage, the gap between my father and me may have been insurmountable. He didn't understand what it meant to be an American child growing up in the 1990s. I didn't understand what it meant to be a child in India. Most important, I didn't understand what it meant to be a father from India to a millennial son here in the United States.

He certainly made a good faith effort, but the execution was iffy and boy, did I resent him for it. Year after year, my dad showed up to my Little League games without understanding the rules. I struck out early and often. One time, I swear I saw him standing up and cheering for me after I struck out. I am fairly positive that he thought that's what was supposed to happen. (*My son doesn't have to endure the punishment of running the bases!*)

But my career didn't make much sense to an electrical engineer from India. He knows that I am a journalist and a writer for the *New York Times*—but what that means has always been something foreign to him.

Bishakha understood a bit more, but not too much. Growing up, the television she approved of me watching, outside of *7th Heaven* of course, was the news. She didn't understand what went into a broadcast, but she loved Peter Jennings, the ABC anchor. She liked *20/20* and *60 Minutes*. She was a news consumer in a way my father wasn't. This probably wasn't Bishakha's intent, but her appreciation for the news probably nudged me toward being a reporter.

When I first started at Boston University, my goal was to become a sports broadcaster. I wanted to be the next Bob Costas and call NBA Finals games on television. I was never any good at sports, so this was the next best thing. When I watched games on television, I would mute the television and broadcast the games myself. I would do the same when playing a video game, say *NHL 94* on Sega Genesis.

Eventually, I became a bit bored by sports and shifted to hard news. I was the sports director of the college radio station at BU and found myself disillusioned by just how *regular* athletes are. They sometimes want to show up late for work and act cranky. *Look, Ma! They're just like us.*

After college, my career took several detours—let's call them forced detours—including stops at the *Boston Globe* (didn't renew my contract), NBC (layoff), Al Jazeera (layoff), and Major League Baseball (this was fine). And then I landed the job of a lifetime in 2015: I was tapped to be a campaign reporter for CBS News.

One of the candidates I was initially assigned? Donald J. Trump. My initial reaction? *I won't have to cover that guy at all.*

Woooo, boy. Was I wrong.

I was part of a small group of about five to ten reporters that followed the Trump campaign from start to finish—"embeds," in industry parlance. We went to more than forty states and hundreds of rallies. Trump even sent some angry tweets my way once, calling me and my friend Katy Tur, an NBC reporter, "3rd rate" and "dishonest," adding that we should be fired. I'm sure he was just joking.

Shyamal didn't know what it meant to be a campaign embed for a national television network. *Are you on television?* Sometimes. *So you're a cameraman?* Sometimes. *You write stories?* Sometimes. *I don't get it.* I know.

Covering the Trump campaign made me hyperaware of just how brown I am, with or without family ties. No matter how American I felt as an Indian-American, for some, the hyphen mattered more. The political press corps is almost entirely white, to say nothing about the demographics of Trump's rally crowds.

At a rally in Las Vegas, Nevada, an older white man came up

to me as I was doing an interview and yelled that I should go back to Iraq where I came from.

I am, of course, not from Iraq. That gentleman meant Howell, New Jersey! Although "Go back to New Jersey where you came from!" might be the worse insult.

Weeks later, the press corps was in Reno. There was a huge line outside the ballroom where Trump was slated to speak. See, that was the thing about Trump rallies: There were always long lines. He wasn't doing rallies in diners and coffee shops. He was doing them in basketball arenas. People would line up the night before to get a good seat. His supporters would show up dressed like him and holding signs. It was like Republican political Woodstock. I met Trump supporters who would travel around the country, going to every rally. Trump was the political equivalent of the Allman Brothers. Every show was different, and just like the band, some songs would meander on without end.

I was taking pictures of the line outside of the Reno rally when another older white man, this one wearing an outfit with Vietnam patches on it, said to me, "Hey, what are you doing? Shooting photos for ISIS?"

How could someone be that brazen in public? I was furious. First, I was mad about the racism. Second, really? Crowd photos? I'm, what, an intern for ISIS? Not even senior management? My goodness. Systemic discrimination exists in places you don't expect.

I maintained my professionalism and finished what I was doing. Afterward, I walked up to him and said, "Sir, just so you know, I'm not a member of ISIS. I work for CBS News." He threw his hands up, as if I was attacking him, and said, "I don't know who you are. Be glad you're born in this country."

Sir, I am. Because I have the freedom to call you an asshole in a book. *You're an asshole.*

But my skin color never felt as hot as it did when the Trump campaign went to Chicago.

Oftentimes, as a reporter chasing Trump on the trail, you couldn't help but feel like you were pursuing a carnival disguised as a presidential campaign. It was a big shiny object. Look, there is Trump giving out Senator Lindsey Graham's phone number! (This happened.) Look, there's an elephant! No, a real elephant! (There actually once was a real elephant outside of a Trump rally.) Oh my . . . Trump just joked in front of thousands of people that a supporter's wife was fantasizing about him in bed! (Yes, this happened.) Is that someone dressed like a southern border wall? That's not even the weirdest thing I've seen today, because there's a man dressed like Colonel Sanders about a hundred feet away. (Both things happened.)

Protesters were a mainstay of Trump rallies, and by March 2016, tempers were at a fever pitch. By this time, Trump was the dominant front-runner in the Republican Party, not just because of high polling but because of actual wins. He had won the New Hampshire and South Carolina primaries by large margins, in addition to the Nevada caucuses. He was winning so much that, as he put it, "your heads will spin."

One of the big storylines floating around Trump's candidacy was the amount of violence at his rallies, which many accused Trump of encouraging.

I watched hundreds, if not a couple of thousand, protesters get ejected from Trump rallies over the course of being an embed. It usually went the same way: The protesters made noise. The crowd jeered. Trump yelled, "Get 'em out!" Then he'd go on an extended riff blasting the protesters, maybe mocking them ("Go home to Mommy!"), maybe encouraging supporters to physically harm them ("If you see somebody getting ready to throw a tomato, knock the crap out of 'em."), maybe inviting peace ("Don't hurt 'em!"). The protesters were escorted out. The rally (and the show) went on. We were used to this.

Trump was supposed to have a rally in Chicago on March 11, 2016. As soon as it was announced, the chatter of massive protests started making the rounds. A week earlier, Trump addressed a packed airport hangar outside New Orleans, and as he started speaking, he held up, Lion King–style, a baby he had signed in Baton Rouge at an earlier rally. Just in case your eyes glossed over that last sentence, he held up a baby he'd autographed—with an actual marker—weeks before as if he was Baby Simba in *The Lion King*.

This Chicago rally was supposed to be held at the UIC Pavilion on the University of Illinois at Chicago campus. As I entered the arena hours beforehand, the intensity was already palpable. Hundreds of yelling and chanting young protesters had taken over nearly the entire back half of the arena. Perhaps out of familiarity or wishful thinking, I mentally played down the reports that there would be large-scale protests. *This happens at every rally.* But it was another reporter standing near me who made me reconsider. Surveying the back of the room, she remarked, "Some shit is gonna go down tonight." I chuckled uneasily, realizing, somewhere in the back of my mind, that she was probably right. This was more reality than carnival.

The night started off normally enough when three men wearing white T-shirts were ejected in an upper section of the arena. I jetted toward them with my camera to grab footage, just in case it got rowdy. Their T-shirts read MUSLIMS UNITED AGAINST TRUMP on the back, and as the crowd chanted, "U-S-A!" each man raised one fist into the air. No violence. There was an order to these things. Like clockwork. They were escorted out under an electronic scoreboard reading MAKE AMERICA GREAT AGAIN.

I remarked to a Slate reporter, "People think it's new, but this has been going on at Trump rallies since at least November. There'll be ten more of those tonight." The back of my mind hadn't reached the front of my lips.

What I didn't realize was that hundreds of protesters had gathered outside. Cable news was running constant aerials of the crammed streets. The intensity started ramping up, both inside and outside the arena. Eventually, much to the shock of all of us, Trump canceled the rally about half an hour before it was supposed to start, setting off pandemonium unlike anything I had ever seen.

Scuffles started breaking out inside and outside, and protests were becoming violent as demonstrators clashed with police. I grabbed my camera and ran outside to gather footage for the network.

Suddenly, in a split second, I felt a tug on the back of my sweatshirt. Well, it wasn't so much of a tug as it was an aggressive backward yank from multiple police officers.

"Whoa, whoa, whoa, whoa, whoa!" I yelled.

I was slammed into the ground.

"Put your hands behind your back! Hands behind your back!"

My face was bashed into the street. My camera went flying. One of the officers put his boot to my neck and handcuffed me. I could hear nothing at this point other than the sound of the arresting officer's police walkie-talkie blaring codes.

The police officer walked away. I lay there on the street on my stomach, in shock. The entire process took about thirty seconds; I never even saw the police officers' faces. I just knew I was in pain and that a mistake had been made. Another officer eventually came and picked me up off the ground and escorted me to the police van. I calmly informed him that I was a member of the press and asked why I had been arrested. He (very genuinely, I think) said he didn't know. For the next couple of hours, I was in police custody. I was able to, however—somehow, while handcuffed—reach into my pocket, grab my phone, and alert the higher-ups at the network that I had been arrested.

Word spread like wildfire that I was detained. It turned out that Fox News had run video of my arrest without realizing I was a journalist, which ended up being what saved me. You see, no one could seem to explain exactly why I had been thrown to the ground and handcuffed. I wasn't doing anything wrong. I didn't disobey any police officers. I was a journalist on a public street doing my thing. So I was bizarrely charged with resisting arrest. Aside from the Fox News footage, my camera continued to roll. You could clearly hear me very politely asking a Chicago police officer why I had been arrested.

An unexpected highlight: The camera was in a police officer's hand and still rolling while I was in the police van. When I retrieved the camera later, I played back the footage and heard one officer ask another about the camera. The other replied, "It belongs to one of these dickheads."

One of these dickheads. Please put that on my tombstone.

The footage is what led the CPD to drop the charges a couple of days later. I feel certain that if Fox News knew this would happen, they would not have aired my arrest. (In a weird moment, I found out the charges were dropped because a reporter from CNN called me to ask for comment. No wonder the network bills itself as the home for breaking news.)

I was asked recently if I was scared that night. To be perfectly honest, I wasn't. Not because I am the epitome of bravery or anything like that. Simply put, I was baffled. The entire time, whether I was on my stomach with my face looking at concrete or in the police van, I thought repeatedly: *This is a huge mistake and someone is going to come along and clear this up any minute now.* On top of that, I was focused on my job. I had footage to feed. It didn't hit me how serious and potentially dangerous the situation was. During that first hour after the arrest, I was frustrated to be kept from doing the task I was in Chicago to do.

But in the meantime, I was sent to jail. I was let out later that night, and by that point, the story had gone viral. CBS ran multiple stories about the incident. My phone was blowing up with text messages, calls, and emails. Hungry reporters wanted me to comment on being unjustly arrested. Me? I was just hungry. I wanted to go to bed.

I called my bosses at CBS to fill them in on what had happened, then went to the network's satellite truck and fed all my footage to the New York headquarters. In the process, I rewatched the incident from the vantage point of my camera.

After a precautionary trip to the hospital, I went to my hotel room, flipped my phone to silent, and went to sleep.

You might notice a missing sentence in there. Well, I did something stupid. Or, rather, I *didn't* do something: I forgot to tell my family what had happened. I was so tired that it didn't even occur to me. When I got back to my hotel room, I wanted nothing more than for my head to hit the pillow. I didn't want to discuss the incident or relive it. I wasn't traumatized—many journalists have been through much worse—but it was not something I had ever experienced before.

I figured I would get in touch with my folks in the morning. And honestly, the last thing you want to do as a child of brown parents is to call and tell them that you've been arrested.

I can just imagine it now.

ME: Hey Ma, listen. I'm calling you from jail—

BISHAKHA: I knew it! I knew this would happen! I told you you should've went to grad school.

ME: No, Ma. It's not like that. If you could just listen for a second—

BISHAKHA: What did you do? I bet it was all that drinking and drugging.

ME: What? No, I was—

BISHAKHA: It was sex, wasn't it? You were arrested for sex. I told you to focus on your studies and not the sex stuff!

ME: I can't believe I used my one phone call on this.

The next day, I awoke to a phone call from my father in India. I thought it was going to be one of his catch-up phone calls, where I'd be in for a few long minutes of awkward conversation about the weather.

"WHAT HAPPENED?!" my father yelled into the phone.

I said, "Oh Dad, I am so sorry I didn't tell you. Basically, I was in Chicago and we were here for a Trump rally, and—wait a minute . . . How did you know? You live in India."

He said, "You're in every newspaper in India. MY SON IS A STAR!"

Our car eventually made its way to Shyamal's neighborhood, Salt Lake (basically the Brooklyn of Kolkata), and was slowly meandering to the Hyatt, an imposing marvel hidden behind a thick layer of security. My father began offering a few scant details about the life he had lived since moving here.

"I was very extraordinarily careful about my health. It's very important. Sports. Music. I practice piano, accordion, and vocals," he said. There was more. He said he did yoga. And he played golf, plus tennis three times a week without fail. Jogging.

"Perhaps I haven't told you that I've taken lots of interest in cosmology," he added.

Great, I thought. My dad had moved to India and become a hippie. Maybe he'd like the Dave Matthews Band as much as I do.

"Cosmology? I'm looking forward to hearing about it," I said with a laugh. Would it be too much to ask my father if he would smoke pot with me?

"Nowadays, I'm busy watching the sky with a binocular and everything," Shyamal said, deadly serious. "We have a skywatch club. We meet every Saturday. You go camping twice a year to go outside and watch the planets."

"Do you have a lot of friends?" I asked. I had a feeling I knew what the answer was going to be.

"No," he said. He wasn't irked by it. He was matter-of-fact, like he was when telling me about the writer Rabindranath Tagore.

"To be honest with you, I am my friend. And my accordion. And my piano. My binocular. And my books. My art collections. They are my friends," my father said.

But Dad, I wanted to say, *those are just things.* But I don't think he knew the difference. I'm not sure he ever had a friend.

"I lead a very disciplined life. Very careful life. I'm okay. Full of spirit," he said.

Full of spirit. On this, he was right. If there was one thing he had, much to my surprise, it was spirit. This level of rejuvenation had been unforeseen on my end. I had spent the last eleven years looking for my own place in the world, and it appeared that Shyamal had been looking for his.

FIVE

"Sent from my iPad."

The next morning, exhausted from the flight but anticipating what lay ahead, I woke up to an email from Bishakha.

> Subject: Hi shambo, are you and Wesley enjoying the city, what have you seen so far.
> Body: What kind of food are you eating, please send some photos, have fun and enjoy. Give my love to Wesley. Ma.

And underneath? "Sent from my iPad."

Bishakha had come a long way since I was in college. During that period, we'd exchange phone calls once every couple of weeks, which was as far as her technological literacy had expanded, given that she never learned how to use a computer. The calls were warmer than the ones with Shyamal, and I always felt a bit more sympathetic toward her because she was the human equivalent of analog in a digital world. It's hard to live in the United States without being technologically fluent—say, not knowing how to send an email. Shyamal never had that problem. (Plus Shyamal was the one who had moved away with no explanation.)

In 2009, my junior year, I had been accepted into Boston University's study-abroad program in London. I was going to be a radio reporter for the spring semester at a small station called Hayes FM, and it would also be my first time going to Europe. It was going to be difficult for Bishakha and me to talk on the phone, both financially and logistically.

She asked me to teach her how to use email over winter break.

I was skeptical that this would work. My mother didn't know how to turn on the computer, let alone type, navigate browsers, or use passwords, and, at the time, a cable modem. We forget that there was a time when wireless routers weren't the norm.

But we gave it a shot.

Every day during winter break, I sat down with Bishakha at the desktop computer in the basement of our home in Howell. We created an email address for her with a simple password, and I showed her where to place her hands on the keyboard. She would insist on typing only with the pointer finger on each hand: a painstaking process. We would get very frustrated with each other. I would lose patience with her inability to grasp simple concepts, like double clicking. She would get irritated with my tone. There was an extra annoyance on my end because I knew my white friends' parents knew how to use computers.

Bishakha made progress—slowly. It was a little like when all the famous figures from the past discover a mall in *Bill & Ted's Excellent Adventure*. She was exploring this world she had never tapped into before, and there was a genuine sense of wonderment about all the fascinating things you can do on the Internet. (I didn't introduce her to *all* the things on the Internet, of course.)

I tried teaching her how to use instant messaging on Google, which she found fascinating. But her favorite thing about using the computer was the CAPS LOCK key. She loved typing in capital letters, the same way my dad likes speaking in them. Bishakha, of course, didn't understand that typing in all caps means you're yelling at someone. And she struggled with the notion of hitting ENTER after whatever she had to say. Her chats would just sit there, aimless, with no one to read them. It was, again, an apt metaphor.

She still needed me to hold her hand from start to finish. *Where's the power button on the computer? Where do I type in the site? What is my email address? Why isn't it doing what I want it to do?*

By the time my mother dropped me off at Newark Airport, I thought it was a futile endeavor. She wouldn't be able to do this without me there.

Yet, lo and behold: When I got off the plane at Heathrow and got to my London lodgings, I had an email waiting for me. It was from Bishakha: "HELLO BABA, HOPE YOU GET TO LONDON OKAY. PLEASE DON'T DRINK."

It must've taken her hours to compose, yet here she was. Bishakha had done it. Eventually, she became, er, slightly more proficient with instant messaging.

Here are exact excerpts from our very first Gchat:

ME: hi mom!
BISHAKHA: hishambo
ME: hi ma
ME: i can't believe you figured this out
ME: i'm in class right now
BISHAKHA: what do thinki am ha ha

And a couple of minutes later:

ME: how do you like your new computer?

BISHAKHA: ilike it but i feel like that i am in dark

ME: what do you mean

ME: dont forget to press enter

ME: are you there

That was the end of that conversation—not unlike my early conversations with Wesley. After I graduated, contact between my mother and me gradually decreased. Before our Mother's Day phone call in 2018, I tried to pinpoint exactly when we last had an extended conversation. I ran a search of all our online chats, and I found the following from 2014, our most recent, from around the time I was starting a job as a field producer for Al Jazeera America. There wasn't much improvement in her typing over five years:

ME: hi ma

BISHAKHA: HI BABU HOW ARE YOU

ME: hi ma how are you?

BISHAKHA: I AM OK HOW IS YOUR WORK

ME: it's going well, it's early so i am trying to get to know everyone. how are you doing?

BISHAKHA: I AM REALLY WORRIED ABOUT YOU WHEN YOU ARE SETTLED WITH YOUR LIFE ITHINK I WILL BE OK

ME: oh mom, everything is fine right now, thank you though. . . . . don't worry

BISHAKHA: I TRY NOT TO WORRY BUT I GUESS ITSAA HABBIT. SO FAR DO LIKE THE PEOPLE

ME: yes mom, do me a favor-hit the caps lock button on the far left side of the keyboard. . . . this way you don't type in all capital letters

BISHAKHA: i am sorry i wnnted type it that way

Soon after that, we ceased communicating, which seems ridiculous, given the tenor of that conversation. What happened? Just months following that last chat, I lost my job at Al Jazeera America when the network initiated mass layoffs. I woke up one morning on a day off, noticed my email wasn't working, showed up at the office, and was told to go next door to the Wyndham New Yorker Hotel near Penn Station, where a line of employees waited for the bad news. I had to embark on yet another sudden job search, a year after being laid off at NBC, when *Rock Center with Brian Williams* was canceled. CBS hired me about six months later for a freelance job producing for CBSN, a new digital streaming network. When CBS picked me up, I was in my midtwenties and one week away from being flat broke. Reaching out to my parents as an emotional refuge wasn't in my bloodstream, and bringing my mother into the loop felt like it would be a burden. I was focused on self-preservation, and I didn't have the patience to explain my situation to someone who didn't understand my industry.

On another level, I didn't want to admit failure, to be that twenty-six-year-old son telling his mother that he had run out of money. In a diary I kept at the time, I wrote that I was "feeling slightly alone," then added, "Mom doesn't even know I lost my job."

In 2015, CBS moved me over to the presidential campaign, which ushered in a new round of life upheaval. As a campaign embed, you don't really sleep. You're always in a politics bubble that even your closest friends have difficulty penetrating, let alone distant parents. And you're always on the road at rallies, debates, conventions, you name it. This wasn't something I could easily talk to Bishakha about, and I didn't have time. I never even told her about the new job, because by then months of noncontact had become a year. Selfishly, I knew that being on the road so much made being there for her in any meaningful way almost impossible. I also knew that as a woman in her approximately late sixties, she was getting to the age where she needed help—say, around the house and with medical issues. She wasn't terribly fluent with technology in a world that increasingly doesn't allow for that. By not calling her, I put myself in an ideal position to ignore that dynamic. I put all my energy into my work, in part because that's what campaign reporting requires but also because other parts of my life felt like distractions.

But relationships being a two-way street, I didn't hear from her either. I did notice that after college, she sounded sadder when we spoke, but she never told me what was wrong. Sometimes, she gave the impression that she didn't *want* to hear from me. Our conversations became more strained as we had trouble finding things to converse about, punctuated by frustrating disputes born from the lack of understanding of each other. The increasingly rare calls were filled with long bouts of silence. By the time I started covering the Trump campaign, she was like an old associate from whom I drifted as I tried to maneuver through a stressful adulthood. I didn't make her a priority, and if I were to guess, this frustrated and hurt Bishakha, who, in turn, went into a cocoon of her own. Part of it, I'm sure, was financial. She was fast approaching retirement. She didn't make much money as a cashier at a pharmacy, and she was worried about her security when she couldn't work any longer. I have another theory: Bishakha was having difficulty with how quickly the world around her was evolving. She would express frustration about completing easy tasks online—say, setting up appointments to renew her green card or other basic Internet chores, which she didn't know how to do. Bishakha couldn't progress as fast as the rest of the world.

I have this old handwritten letter I received in the mail

from Bishakha that came folded in a birthday card. It's on lined notebook paper and is about a page long. I don't know exactly what year it's from, but I estimate it to be from about March 2012, two years before that last Gchat. This came in the midst of a particularly stormy time for our relationship.

I had to move home again to New Jersey after college because I couldn't find work after my *Boston Globe* contract ended, which wasn't surprising given how much the recession had ravaged newsrooms. I was unemployed for several months and fighting through my own millennial frustrations about how the world *owed* me. Three months later, I finally landed at NBC and was able to move out again. I was now living in the Gramercy neighborhood of Manhattan.

This is what her note said:

> *Dear Shambo,*
>
> *Happy Birthday. I hope and wish that whatever you want in your life, you will get it. I always pray for you. When you were a child, you did not have a normal life like others. I wish I could do better for you. But you turned out to be a handsome, young man. And I am very proud of you.*
>
> *Ma*

It's one of the few things I have from my mother, the first and only example of my mother's acknowledgment of the difficulties of our family dynamic.

She struggled with depression as I grew up. It manifested itself in various ways, but whatever form it took, the result was anger and tears. My best reasoning is that she was a deeply isolated and lonely individual, trapped in a failing marriage and getting through her days without feeling unconditionally loved. In

Howell, there wasn't a sizable Indian community for Bishakha to be a part of. There was no escape from the unhappy home for her. Whereas Shyamal had an engineering career he had built over many years, and Sattik and I had college and our careers to look forward to, she had nothing of the sort.

When I was growing up, my mother had trouble containing her frustration on a day-to-day basis. Sometimes she would snap at the flip of a switch over something minor—say if a radio was too loud or a room was too messy for her liking.

Other times, Bishakha's frustration went to a darker place. She would take out her anger on Sattik and me by creating an exceptionally cold dynamic in our childhood home. Coming home from school was like coming back to a roommate who you knew didn't like you; it wasn't bad enough to transfer rooms (or schools!), but you had to wait until graduation.

A therapist I saw once—not Sleeping Jerome—told me his theory about people and relationships. According to him, there are three types of people. There's Type 1, who grows up with some sort of childhood trauma or currently lives within an emotionally challenging environment, which creates an emotional hole in that person. He or she will spend his or her life trying to fill that hole. That's why people might settle for being in relationships they shouldn't be in or putting up with unfortunate behaviors from significant others. There's Type 2, who has those same deficiencies and that same hole, but will protect the hole rather than trying to fill it. The Type 2 won't get close to anyone, and anyone who tries to get close will be pushed away. Type 3 is the well-adjusted person, who may have experienced trauma or may have come from a foundation of love and warmth, but knows in any case how to properly give and accept love.

Bishakha is a Type 2. She pushes people away. She pushed me away by frequently saying that she didn't feel anyone in the world loved her, then going to her room and shutting the door (literally and figuratively). When she was feeling her worst, she made cutting remarks designed to create distance between us. She is, overall, a kind person who has struggled with showing it consistently.

The ultimate expression of warmth among loved ones or friends, outside of saying "I love you," is "How was your day?" I realized that recently, thanks to Wesley. She always inquires about the mundane goings-on of my day, which shows a level of investment in me that would leave a great gap in my life if it no longer existed. On an emotional level, some of the most intimate moments I have had with her resulted from our sharing the *dumbest* things about our lives, not just the big events.

Bishakha never asked me about my day when I was young, nor did I ask her. Shyamal never asked me, and I never asked him. Bishakha and Shyamal never asked each other. Same goes for Sattik with each of us. The Deb family household would have been so much different if we asked each other to run down our respective days, just like my friend Shaun's family did. Instead, the four of us lived in four corners of the house, finding our own outlets for our sadness and clawing at the outside world begging for release.

My family's struggles all came to a head in eighth grade, when I was thirteen. Shyamal, Bishakha, and I were on our way to a family friend's house. And as was characteristic for my father, he got lost. It led to an argument between my parents, which was also normal. But something seemed different about this one. Bishakha and Shyamal were viscerally angrier. My mother was shaking and crying. My father slammed his hand on the steering wheel. Over what? His getting lost? It all seems so silly now. If Shyamal used GPS, would our family have been fine?

When we got home, my mother locked herself in her room.

She stayed there for approximately six months.

I barely saw her for the rest of eighth grade.

She only came out of her room to occasionally make herself food or go to her job at Drug Fair, the pharmacy where she was a cashier. We were all isolated, but this was a level unprecedented in our household. Suddenly Shyamal was thrust into the role of being my primary caretaker. He began cooking and cleaning the house, in addition to his engineering career. It was only then I realized the depths of my mother's depression and, perhaps, her fear of the outside world: She could not bring herself to leave her room to face it.

I was stewing too. I was acting up in class—what I eventually realized was a combination of puberty, trying to make friends, and bafflement about what was happening at home. I didn't check on my mother, perhaps fueling her cycle of belief that no one cared about her. This was, of course, not true. I did care about her. I cared about Shyamal too. But I didn't know what was going on. And I was just trying to get through school.

Shyamal was overwhelmed, dealing with an unruly son with whom he barely had a relationship. I was openly hostile to him, and my petulance, instead of distance, became the defining characteristic of our relationship. For example, I played the piano for our eighth grade musical at Howell Township Middle School South—*My Fair Lady*, I believe—and the cast party after the show was at an Applebee's near our house. I asked Shyamal if I could go. He said no—reasonably so, because it was late and he couldn't come pick me up.

I shrieked. I started throwing papers in our family room. *How could you not let me go? Who are you? You're nothing.* It was totally unacceptable behavior on my part. There was stuff like this every week. Sometimes I would get physically abrasive with Shyamal. I was just so angry all the time. We all were.

I stormed out of the house, even as Shyamal yelled at me not to, and walked to the Applebee's, staying there with the show's cast, munching on mozzarella sticks, boneless buffalo wings, and whatever other chain restaurant appetizers the place had. The party lasted till one in the morning, and I left to walk home. Mind you, I was in eighth grade.

As I left the Applebee's, I heard a honk in the parking lot.

Shyamal was there, waiting in the car. He had been parked there for hours, making sure I didn't have to walk home by myself.

I didn't say a word in the car ride home.

Along with "How was your day?" "I'm sorry" is an essential expression for loved ones. I never said that to my father. I should have apologized to him that night. Or the other nights, when I let my bitterness take hold. I should've said "I'm sorry" to my mother too.

One school night, I was playing on the computer in the basement of our house. The basement was my sanctuary. I never had a Super Nintendo growing up, so I had downloaded an emulator on our desktop that could re-create Nintendo games. It's where I played various versions of Pokémon or straight computer games like *Star Trek: Elite Force* for hours. I had played so voraciously that I got thirsty, so I went upstairs to get a glass of water.

As I emerged at the top of the stairs, I did a double take. There were multiple police officers at my front door and flashing lights outside.

One of them saw me and said, "Did you see what happened?"

Was I dreaming?

I said the first thing that came to my head. "No, did you?" I responded. I thought for a second that something had happened outside and the police were looking for witnesses.

I turned around, and there was Shyamal walking out of our living room, being led into a police car while Bishakha frantically got into her car. She was headed to the station too. The police *were* looking for witnesses—witnesses inside the house. Within minutes, I was by myself.

I never learned what happened, and I don't care to know. It was emblematic of my approach, remaining blind to this massive, traumatic occurrence in my own family. There seemed to have been some sort of confrontation between the two of them, and somebody called the police. It wasn't the first time this had happened in our family, but it hadn't been this bad in many years. I still remember the next morning, taking the bus to school, fielding questions from kids on the bus who wanted to know why the police were at my house. I genuinely didn't know what to tell them.

But this time it marked the end of my parents' tumultuous journey together, a failed experiment that lasted decades longer than it should have. Shyamal and I would never live under the same roof again; my parents officially divorced when I was a junior, roughly three years later.

Bishakha emerged from her bedroom and reasserted herself in the household, away from the stresses of a failing marriage. Shyamal was living in an apartment a short drive away. Both, perhaps feeling a taste of freedom, made earnest attempts to connect with me. Shyamal took me out to eat once every couple of weeks. Usually we'd get Chinese. You know what he'd say?

"How was your day?"

I didn't appreciate it then, but now I realize that he was trying. So was my mother, who gleefully attended the high school musicals of which I was a part. Not that she couldn't before. She just seemed happier now.

Meanwhile I started living life, essentially, on my own. I stopped caring about what my relationship was with them. A friend of mine who had his license taught me how to drive. When I was fifteen, I got a job at Pathmark, a local grocery store, and eventually saved up eight hundred dollars to buy a 1998 Ford Escort with faulty brakes. I crashed it within weeks. So I saved up another eight hundred to buy a 1989 Honda Accord with 150,000 miles on it. During senior year of high school, I crashed that one too, by absentmindedly driving into a fence by the track field. Then came another eight hundred, and this time the car was a relatively recent 2002 Chevy Cavalier.

As often as I could, I'd drive away from the house. (I know, I should've stopped driving.) I'd go to the mall. Go to Applebee's. Starbucks. The movies. Whatever. I worked several different retail jobs, and started dating.

I was ready to be away from both of them, just as they were both ready to reconnect with me, at least as best as they knew how. With Shyamal, it was the dinners. With my mother, it was being out of her room.

In 2016, I heard from Bishakha twice: Once was after I was arrested covering the Trump campaign, when she called the next day and told me she was worried sick; and the second was when I got the job at the *Times*. She had received wind of the press release that went out announcing the hire and wanted to congratulate me. Both conversations lasted only minutes. In the case of the Trump arrest, I assured her I was fine but that I had to go.

It meant a lot that she would reach out, but I was not in a headspace to fully reintegrate her into my life. The stresses of covering a presidential campaign did not allow for emotional family reunions. I didn't get there with her till that fateful Mother's Day of 2018, when I *finally* picked up the phone to call her and set a lunch date.

I didn't know it at the time, but Bishakha's apartment is very similar to Shyamal's in India. It is on the second floor of an apartment complex just off Route 9, a busy highway that runs through various suburban New Jersey towns and is referenced in Bruce Springsteen's "Born to Run." There was a golf course adjacent to the complex, although I was certain that my mother wasn't the type to don a golf cap and grab a nine-iron.

As Wesley and I got to Bishakha's door, I took a deep breath, then knocked three times. The door wasn't locked, so I let us in.

"Hello?" I said.

I heard a voice in another room.

"I'll call you back. Shambo is here," Bishakha said.

My mother emerged, with a high-pitched singsong voice, and a slight limp.

"Hi Baba! How are you, Sona?" she said, using another pet name, roughly translating to "my precious" (not like Gollum).

"I'm good. Hi Mom," I said.

Bishakha started speaking in Bengali. "Oh my god. How many days has it been since I've seen you?" she said, before enveloping me in a big embrace. She let out a deep sigh as she hugged my waist. I am probably a foot taller than her. With her arms clinging to me like barnacles, she asked me how everything was going.

Well, Mother, if you must know. I decided to embark on a journey to reconnect with both of my parents with whom I had virtually no relationship growing up. One moved to a foreign country without telling me and one has me in a bear hug as we speak.

"Good. This is Wesley," I said, indicating my savior, who

seemed not to mind drifting into the background.

"Hello, Wesley! How are you?" Bishakha immediately let me go and turned her embraceable arms toward Wesley.

"It's so nice to meet you," Wesley said.

We handed Bishakha the homemade double-chocolate crinkle cookies and flowers we brought for her.

"Oh yeah! Thank you! I'm so glad you could come. I'm really so happy to see you. Please sit down. Are you guys hungry?" she said. Her voice was sharp. I wondered when was the last time she had received any gifts from anybody.

Bishakha began preparing lunch. She had made my favorite mustard fish curry from when I was a child. I was struck by how empty her apartment looked: There was barely any art on the walls, and some shelves had nothing on them. There were no pictures of Sattik or me, or anyone at all. It was almost like no one had been here for months. My childhood piano was still there.

Her apartment had two bedrooms. I remember visiting once when she first moved here, probably around five years prior. There was a cozy porch where Bishakha said she read books. She also said she often took walks around the neighborhood for exercise.

"Oh Sopan, can you do me a favor?" I heard Bishakha say from the kitchen. "Remember my phone? It's an old phone number?"

I wasn't sure what she meant.

"What do you need me to do?" I said.

"Change the voicemail with a new number. Please?" my mother said.

Bishakha's home phone voicemail was my voice talking about an old phone number. She had never changed it because I don't think she knew how. We did it for her. Bishakha insisted that Wesley's voice should greet her callers now. So Wesley, along with a plethora of other talents, became a voiceover artist.

"It's a little spicy, isn't it?" Bishakha said, doting on Wesley as we began to eat in her dining room. Wesley and I sat on one side of the table, with my mother on the opposite.

"It's really good," Wesley said.

"You like it?" Bishakha beamed.

"Mmhmm." Wesley nodded.

Bishakha kept bringing out plates of food. There was enough to feed an entire Little League team in one sitting.

"He doesn't come at all. So, you know, I want him to eat something I cook," Bishakha said, referring to me. "Of course, you're coming and I want you to eat too. I wasn't sure if you'd like the food I cook. I don't cook these days at all. I'm by myself. I really don't have to cook."

"It's really good, Mom. You haven't lost your touch," I answered, looking down at my plate.

At first, lunch was a bit like those *Saturday Night Live* sketches with Will Ferrell, where he plays a middle manager who yells at his family about owning a Dodge Stratus. One of the brilliant comic bits of the skit is that there are long pockets of silence punctuated solely by the sound of utensils loudly clattering against plates. The rest of the sketch is filled with mundane small talk.

Wesley and I told Bishakha about a recent trip to Charleston to visit Wesley's family, when I went fishing for the first time. We talked about Wesley's cooking skills and how she sets off the fire alarm every time she makes a meal. Bishakha said she knew her next-door neighbor who was "very nice."

"Rest of them, they aren't very friendly," she said.

More clattering. I sampled the shrimp.

"You should come time to time to have my food. Then I can cook again," Bishakha said.

Wesley and I took another serving. I was going to need another run in the morning.

"So you have an iPad?" I asked.

"I like it. My computer is gone," Bishakha answered. She said her laptop had stopped working about five years ago. But she didn't like reading books on the iPad because she liked physically touching book pages.

Bishakha glanced at Wesley. Her next question made me flinch for a split second.

"Can I ask a personal question, if you don't mind? How did you meet Sopan?" Bishakha said.

She had never shown this level of interest in a significant other of mine. Recall that when I approached her with my sixth grade romance, she laughed it off and then we never discussed women again. She had met Michelle, my college girlfriend, once over a similar lunch in 2011. It was awkward. They didn't click, through nobody's fault. No one really knew how to act, including me. Neither of us were ready to open ourselves up. I didn't realize until now that introducing parents to a significant other does require willingness, acceptance, and transparency.

Here Bishakha was, in front of someone with whom I'm romantically involved, asking her questions about that romance.

Wesley recounted how we'd met through Twitter.

"Do you know what Twitter is?" I asked Bishakha.

"Mmhmm. I don't tweet but I know what it is," Bishakha said. Talk about an evolution: from not knowing how to turn on a computer to *understanding* Twitter—though, really, who can ever understand such a thing?

"She has an iPad, babe," Wesley said. A fair point. I began to wonder if my mother was about to ask me what my favorite hashtag was. We told Bishakha that Wesley was finishing up law school when we met, which I had mentioned on the phone.

"Oh, you're a lawyer?" Bishakha said, her eyebrows raised. "Good."

We moved on to discussing politics, something my mother and I had never done.

"These days, I don't enjoy politics at all," Bishakha said. "I used to enjoy watching what's going on. It's not news anymore. I used to love Charlie Rose. I used to watch every day."

No longer. She added that she never liked Matt Lauer from the start. My mother, the media critic, said that the news had become too gossipy.

I told Bishakha that Trump had tweeted at me because he wasn't a fan of a story I wrote.

"What's wrong with you?" Bishakha said, with the belly laugh I hadn't heard in years. "Oh my, you're on a hit list! I remember that he made a very nasty comment about Meryl Streep."

We finished lunch and cleared the dishes. I was feeling more comfortable than I had been when we first arrived. There was some chatting in my mother's living room as we ate the cookies we'd brought. Bishakha asked if we wanted to take the piano, adding that she had no use for it, but there was no way we could give it a home in our small Manhattan apartment.

I had never seen my mother this happy. She insisted on taking a picture with Wesley. She took one with me too, but honestly, Bishakha seemed more excited about Wesley. I wasn't complaining. I was just happy lunch went well.

On the car ride back, I had this gnawing feeling that I couldn't shake. It made me grip the steering wheel harder.

"She lives a very sad life," I said to Wesley, as we cruised the highway back to New York. No amount of one-off lunches would reduce my guilt about her having been by herself this whole time.

"She seemed really happy to have us there," Wesley countered. She was right: Bishakha was happy when we were there. She was warm and embracing toward Wesley. And now Wesley's voice was Bishakha's phone greeting.

"I've never seen her like that around any of my friends," I said.

"Do you know when her birthday is?" Wesley asked. I didn't. I must've known at some point. I didn't know Shyamal's either.

"She doesn't strike me as someone who sees value in things anymore," I said. "The place is empty pretty much."

When you visit someone's home, you learn a lot about their biography just by what's on their walls: the art they like, the family trips they've taken, their diplomas—even the very color of the wall symbolizes something. Bishakha's walls were a pasty white, mostly bare, save for a smattering of muted paintings. Her home was a blank slate that would tell a stranger nothing about the occupant.

At some point, I'd have to learn what was *supposed* to be on my mother's walls. And most important: Why wasn't I on them?

SIX

"To them, he is a common man."

"Do you have a goal in front of you? What you want to do next?" my father asked. We were strolling outside the complex of Belur Math, a sprawling forty-acre area located near Kolkata on a distributary of the Ganges River.

Shyamal, as I discovered on this trip, had a particular fascination with old temples and forts and was intent on showing us every one of them, along the way explaining their significance. It was monsoon season in Kolkata, meaning every second outdoors was hot and humid, ideal for long lectures about old Mughal invasions. All about the Mughals, this guy.

This series of striking temples, conceived by Swami Vivekananda, was stunning. Vivekananda, born Narendranath Datta in Kolkata in 1863, was the son of a lawyer and eventually became a famed monk. Known for his acceptance of all faiths, he delivered a notable speech in 1893 at the Parliament of the World's Religions, an interfaith assembly in Chicago, where he extolled the virtues of tolerance and truth.

I could see why Shyamal would find this place an object of fascination. It emphasized agency. You can be who you want, whenever you want. It was unfamiliar territory for a man who, I would come to learn, was given little choice his entire life.

"What do I want to do next?" I repeated his question back to him. "I don't know, Dad. I'd like to . . ."

I didn't have a good answer. At that moment, my only goal was to make it to dinner without melting from the heat. In the long term, my future is something I've thought about every day for years and have never come up with a satisfactory answer. I have always gone from job to job, figuring it out as I go. And short-term goals have sometimes been sidelined, orphaned by layoffs and my own impulsivity. I get easily attached and invested in side projects: *I am going to write a play and stage it Off Broadway*. And then easily detached a short time later: *Eh, who goes to see plays nowadays?*

"I might go into comedy more after this. Maybe write a television show," I volunteered.

"So you're a comedian?" He smiled. "I find that you have two qualities of mine that you have inherited. One is music. The other is comedy."

"Yeah? You think I inherited comedy from you?" I said, dubious.

"Of COURSE!" my dad squealed. "Whenever I have gone to the parties and all these things, I am the main focus. Even now."

"Is that right?" I said.

"EVEN NOW! Telling the jokes. Making people laugh—that is my hobby."

If you're wondering about my skepticism, it was because the father I knew growing up was the least funny person I had ever met. He never once made me or anyone around me laugh. I have little memory of him even smiling or making anyone else smile. He was more likely to be the class frown than the class clown. If I had inherited my comedy from him, it would explain the number of times I've bombed a set. So, *thanks,* Dad.

Off in the distance, we could see the central Ramakrishna Temple, a grand building combining several different architectural styles, as if to adhere to Vivekananda's vision of inclusiveness. There were domes of different sizes scattered across the top of the elegantly designed structure, made up chiefly of marble and wood. It was roughly a hundred feet tall and had a pinkish-red color. Monkeys roamed the grounds, crisscrossing among delighted tourists and locals who ignored them.

Wesley, Shyamal, and I took our shoes off and went inside the temple, where it was nearly silent, save for the shuffling of feet and the occasional whisper. Several visitors were on their knees with their eyes closed in front of a marble carving of Ramakrishna, the celebrated nineteenth-century spiritual figure who spent his life contemplating the divinity of several religions and his belief in the Supreme Being. I found the atmosphere inside the temple peaceful rather than spiritual, perhaps owing to my agnosticism. Shyamal took delicate steps around the temple, separate from Wesley and me. I couldn't figure out what he was thinking, whether he was recalling Ramakrishna's teachings himself or not.

Finding myself in a contemplative state, I briefly considered that maybe I had dismissed Shyamal being one of my unwitting comedic influences too quickly. After all, as an engineer, part of his job was to try and use logic to overcome complex puzzles. It required an analytical mind to excel at solving them. That's not *too* far off from comedians who point out logical fallacies and search for the right punchline.

Maybe that was a stretch.

Shyamal had one more sight to show us after we had left the temple. He beckoned us to follow him to the banks of the Ganges as the sun went down. For forty-five minutes, we stood on the water's edge, taking in the beautiful landscape as the sky became darker. We watched as several locals dove into the water for a swim. We weren't inside the temple anymore, but we remained silent. It was peaceful. It was perfect.

The trip to Belur Math offered a window into my father and his idiosyncrasies. But it took a while after we first arrived to find our rhythm. Those first two or three days felt like weeks. On our first morning, Shyamal picked us up at our hotel. We didn't get much sleep the night before; I had woken up at about four in the morning and gone for a run to reduce both my anxiety and that weight gain my father kept pointing out. Shyamal took us to the tennis courts where he played three times a week, where he could quickly show us around and show us off. Every Monday, Wednesday, and Friday, he woke up at six o'clock to go play. I met his coach, who has worked with him for the last ten years. There was a nice bit of irony here: I grew up obsessed with sports and grew distant from my father because he and I couldn't bond over it. He moves to India and spends a decade trying to become Pete Sampras.

We got back in the car as instructed with little idea what would be on the day's agenda. Shyamal had it all carefully planned, but we had difficulty convincing him to reveal his plans more than five minutes in advance.

We pulled over on a shady residential street, and a familiar face jumped into the backseat with me and Wesley: my cousin Susmita. I didn't know she would be here and I hadn't seen her in roughly twenty years. She is married to Shyamal's nephew, Somnath, and the two live in Connecticut with their two children, both of whom were attending the University of Connecticut.

Susmita and Somnath had an arranged marriage in 1992, although their relationship is a healthy one, the ideal for what my parents' was supposed to be. Trisha and Ron, their well-adjusted children who grew up in the United States, come to India regularly.

So to recap: Shyamal, my father, has an older brother, Sudhirendra. Sudhirendra's son, Somnath (Shyamal's nephew), married Susmita. (There are lots of names that start with S in my family.) Don't worry, I couldn't yet follow the branches of this family tree, either. I had always assumed that my father was Somnath's uncle in the colloquial sense, just a family friend.

"I can't even—that same face!" Susmita said, greeting me.

It turned out she happened to be in town for the summer because Somnath's father was in poor health. There was a contrast here right from the start: My father told me he had been sick, although I didn't know with what, when I told him I was coming to India. I hadn't known he was sick. And even if I had, what would I have done? When Somnath and Susmita found out about Somnath's father, Susmita made immediate plans to come to India. I could not imagine rearranging my life to look after Shyamal.

Shyamal and Susmita took Wesley and me to the shop of a local tailor. Before our arrival in India, Shyamal had bought Wesley a cherry-red lehenga and a turquoise sari to wear to Manvi's wedding. He had Susmita pick them out because he didn't trust his own fashion sense. They had made arrangements to get Wesley fitted—in the clothes she hadn't ordered!—in case alterations were needed before the wedding.

Over and over again, Shyamal said to us, "You cannot imagine what the wedding in Bengaluru will be. HUUUUUUUUUGE!"

I sat in the lobby of the tiny store as poor Wesley went to the back to disrobe and be poked and prodded and tugged at by strangers speaking in a language she didn't understand. She said they handed her a small, well-worn scrap of fabric and gestured for her to put it on as they measured her mostly naked torso. The process was, in her words, sticky and unpleasant.

Afterward, we went to the mall, and Shyamal made it clear that he intended on spoiling us. He bought me a black pyjama for the wedding and then took us to a jewelry store. He asked Wesley to pick out a pair of earrings and matching necklace.

It reminded me of when I was really young and we lived in the two-bedroom apartment in Randolph. My father had a spoiling tendency then too. Sometimes Shyamal would go out for errands. Maybe my mother sent him or he needed to pick something up, or maybe he just needed to get out of the house. Occasionally he'd take me, and whenever he did, I'd run right to the section of the store where they had computer games. I was a huge fan of science fiction, and I still am today. I'd spend hours in the aisles staring at the screenshots from games on the back of the case, dreaming of being able to play them at home. In particular, I'd look for *Star Wars* and *Star Trek* games and ask Shyamal to buy them for me. He'd say no. But I was ten. I was smart and persistent, and he didn't like disappointing his son.

"Come on, Baba. Please?"

"No."

"Okay, Baba."

Ten minutes later at the register:

"Okay, Baba, I brought the game to the register. It's here already. Let's just buy it."

"Okay."

If it wasn't a computer game, it was baseball cards. I collected thousands of them through middle school. It would infuriate Bishakha, who thought I was wasting too much time and money on playing computer games or on collecting baseball cards and not spending enough time studying. She wasn't wrong. I don't know where those cards are now. They weren't at my mother's apartment when we visited.

After shopping, Shyamal and I would often go to McDonald's, where Shyamal would buy me a McChicken sandwich. He would get one too, but one time, I remember that he also ordered a cheeseburger without cheese.

The baffled cashier said, "So, you want a hamburger?"

"No," Shyamal said. "I want a cheeseburger without cheese."

He was overthinking it. Sometimes he did that.

At the jewelry store in Kolkata, Wesley picked out a small set of rhinestone and pearl earrings, with the matching necklace. They were small. Shyamal didn't think this befit Wesley, whom he couldn't stop showering with praise.

He asked the owner of the jewelry store if he had bigger, more expensive jewelry he could buy her. Wesley and I explained to Shyamal that the smaller pieces were just fine. He wasn't convinced but eventually relented. He wanted everything to be perfect for us.

We finally went to visit Shyamal's home that afternoon. We pulled past the pink façade and into a carport of sorts. Up one flight of a winding staircase, and he stopped us. We sat on a bench outside his door and took our shoes off.

"Have you read *The Da Vinci Code*?" Shyamal asked Wesley. What an odd question to pose out of nowhere.

Wesley paused and answered in the affirmative.

"Here in India, we have a Da Vinci Code," Shyamal said. Wesley and I traded confused looks. Shyamal had Wesley stand up. The key to his apartment was buried underneath the bench.

Ah, a dad joke. I'd never heard him tell a joke before.

"Relax, relax, relax," Shyamal said as we entered the flat. That was another one of my dad's vocal quirks. Sometimes it was never enough to say a casual thing once. He'd have to say it three times. Instead of, "Come on, let's go," it was, "Come on, come on, come on. Let's go, let's go, let's go."

Once inside, Shyamal offered us a beer. *Fuck yeah.* It was the most important thing I did with Shyamal on our first full day together. He strode confidently across the room with ice-cold Kingfishers, a popular Indian lager brewed in Bengaluru, in hand. I had never shared a drink with my father before. If I played my cards right, we'd be playing beer pong soon. Shyamal, my liver, and I had some catching up to do.

Wesley, Susmita, and I sat down on his living room couch, as he poured the Kingfishers for us, then one for himself. I heard shuffling in the kitchen. It was Suparna, the woman my father had hired seven years before to help him around the house.

"Do you like my flat?" Shyamal said.

"Yes, Dad, it's very nice," I answered.

"Good. Did you know that you're the owner?"

Shyamal meant that literally. This was when he told me that he was going to leave his flat in my name when he passed away. I came to India to reconnect and would be leaving with property.

"Today's lunch is vegetarian lunch," Shyamal said. "You'll have salad. You'll have poori and a special daal. Special vegetarian curry. And then some puddings."

"That's great," I said. I was already buzzed. I may have consumed the Kingfisher a bit too quickly, given the heat, exhaustion, jetlag, and anxiety.

We discussed the plans for the next three weeks in excruciating detail. We would spend a few days in Kolkata before flying to Bengaluru for Manvi's wedding. Then we'd link up with Shyamal again in Delhi. From there, we'd go to Agra to see the Taj Mahal and then to Jaipur. For most of the three weeks, my father would serve as our tour guide. No hour was left unaccounted for in Shyamal's itinerary.

Susmita suggested that Shyamal should take us to the Qutb Minar in Delhi, a thirteenth-century minaret, 240 feet high and made of sandstone. Susmita said it was to signify the first Muslim invasion of India.

"Did we win?" I quipped, filling the nervous lull.

My father really was—true to his word—very disciplined. He told us he had one beer and one glass of scotch a week, no more. His daily lunch was very simple, usually rice with daal and some salad. And he kept himself busy, constantly attending lectures and concerts and traveling around the country when he could.

I remarked to Susmita that Shyamal seemed really active.

Susmita said, "Well, you know, he has to pass the time." Did he ever.

Wesley pointed at a picture on the wall. It showed a young boy and a baby.

"Who is this?" she asked.

"That's me. And my brother, Sattik," I answered. I was a bit astonished, since I had never seen this picture before. My brother and I don't have many shots together, and I wasn't sure where this one was set. Sattik had his arms around me. He's completely bald now, but in the photograph he had thick curly black hair. I had fat cheeks and wasn't using them to smile.

To its left was an older picture of Shyamal golfing. "I am losing my hair, you see it. But I am old enough to lose it," Shyamal said, eyeing the picture. He said it so clinically. He wasn't upset about losing his hair or wistful for his younger days. It was a fact of life. Me? I've got a bald spot that's growing in proportion to the federal deficit. And the bald spot bothers me more. I don't care if the country can't pay its bills. Just let me keep my hair. Don't let me follow in Sattik's footsteps.

During the apartment tour, Shyamal briefly mentioned his brother Sudhirendra to Susmita. I realized she had mentioned him that morning too. My ears perked up. *What brothers? I have never heard of any.* I soon learned that my father had nine siblings growing up, Sudhirendra being his oldest. Six of them were still living. There were nine aunts and uncles that I knew nothing about. Sudhirendra was Susmita's father-in-law, whom she was here to visit. Part of the Kolkata itinerary, Shyamal said, was to go meet Sudhirendra and another one of my uncles, Siddhartha. Both lived near my father's house.

I asked my father later to tell me more about his siblings.

"I have seen nine of them," Shyamal said. He was the second youngest.

"Seen nine of them? What does that mean? Do you have more that you didn't meet?" I said. What an odd way to describe siblings: "seen them," as if they were the *Lord of the Rings* franchise in theaters.

"Yes. One or two miscarried babies and more who died," Shyamal said.

I felt foolish asking this next question: "What do you mean, 'died'?"

"Died at the time of delivery or died through childhood," Shyamal answered. "Delivery or early age. Very common in those days. I have since seen nine of them."

The Deb children are listed here—dates and years are estimates, according to Shyamal:

Brothers:

1. Somorendra Kumar Deb (died at twenty-three in 1948)
2. Sudhirendra Kumar Deb (Somnath's father)
3. Hitendra Kumar Deb (died at sixty-eight in 2001)

4. Amal Kanti Deb
5. Arun Kanti Deb
6. Shyamal Kanti Deb
7. Siddhartha Kumar Deb

Sisters:
1. Satadal Deb (died at seventy-six in 2005)
2. Basanti Sarker (died at seventy-eight in 2011)
3. Anjali Dutta

I must have always known Shyamal had brothers and sisters. Where else could Somnath have come from? But as my family splintered, I didn't put much thought into the deeper connection, which seems silly in hindsight. The only sibling who moved to the United States was Shyamal.

"So, show me around," I said. "Give me the tour."

"Pardon me?" Shyamal said.

"Tour! Tour!" Susmita said. "*Dhekye-dhou!*"

"Come on! It's all yours!" Shyamal said.

The apartment had one bedroom, an office, and another room featuring an upright piano. Each room was largely devoid of personal effects but littered with art, books, and small figurines on every surface. He took us into the office, which was simple, cozy, and just bigger than a closet. Here my father quizzed me more about my comedy career. I told him I had performed several shows at the Magnet.

"On Broadway?" Shyamal asked excitedly.

"No, it's not Broadway. It's Off-Off-Off-Off-Off-Off Broadway," I said, lowering expectations as much as I could.

"But you're known," Shyamal said.

"I wouldn't say I'm known," I responded.

Shyamal said that while Googling me, he had found an old picture of me onstage. But how had he known it was old?

"You looked skinnier," Shyamal said, matter-of-factly.

This guy: Maybe he really was the class clown.

In the room with the piano, Shyamal sat me down and made me play. He hadn't heard me play since high school, when I used to perform in the pit band for Howell High School's musicals. I ripped through Billy Joel's "New York State of Mind" and then made my way through some improvised jams on the slightly out-of-tune piano. He used an old point-and-shoot camera to meticulously shoot video of me playing.

"Wow," Shyamal said. But he said it in his Shyamal way. "Wowwwwww."

Out of the corner of my eye, I noticed a photo with a familiar face hanging on a wall next to the piano. I *knew* I had seen that face before. Maybe a relative? Another uncle I hadn't heard of? I couldn't quite place it. *Who was it?* I thought as I blasted through another improvised bit. It was of a man with a striking, confident look. After I had finished my made-up progression, I pointed toward the hanging frame and asked Shyamal who it was. He scoffed, as if I should've known: It was a picture of the actor Omar Sharif, who died in 2015. He was a lead in *Lawrence of Arabia* and *Doctor Zhivago*, and during the 1960s and 1970s he was one of the biggest movie stars in the world. Many prominent actors, particularly in Egypt and around the Middle East, have cited him as a seminal influence.

Here I must make a disclosure. I'm about to tell you the story of why my father hung this photograph in his flat. It is so out of character that I don't actually know if it's true. But I'm going to tell you anyway because I want to believe it's true, and I don't have any reason to think otherwise—other than, of course, its sheer ridiculousness.

Shyamal, in talking about his past, is very unemotional. His stories read as a recitation of facts and figures, devoid of spirit and sentiment. Even the way he described his siblings earlier, including the ones who had died during childbirth, was so unemotional. My father never cared about meeting celebrities. Shyamal was more interested in chemists and their work than actors. He was always unplugged from pop culture, so it's something we never really discussed when I was younger. We had never once discussed our favorite movies or music.

In eighth grade, he did take me to see *Zoolander*. He said afterward, "I didn't understand some of that stuff. Like where they were swinging around."

Shyamal was referring to the orgy scene.

In spite of his apparent lack of interest in celebrity, the reason my father hung the Sharif picture on his wall is that he's a fan and wanted to honor him after he died. This *isn't* the surprising part, though. Many people hang up photos of people they like, though, by my estimation, many of them are not also grown adults. The weird part was told to us over more drinks.

In 2007, when my father abruptly decided to move back to India, the cheapest flight he could get was one that would take him through Cairo and then on to Mumbai and finally Kolkata. When he arrived in Cairo, my father was in ill health, the specific nature of which I'd find out about later. The airport had a doctor who examined him and told him he should rest for a couple of days before continuing to India. As my father told me this story, I didn't press on the nature of his ailment. He had a habit of drifting off topic, and I was determined to hear this.

Though he wasn't well enough to travel, he was apparently well enough to entertain fantasies. Shyamal had heard that Sharif lived in Cairo. He flagged down a cabdriver and asked him if he knew where Sharif lived. My father wanted to touch Sharif's feet, a show of respect for Hindus.

"To them, he is a common man," Shyamal told me in his apartment, as if he was answering for the absurdity of his question.

The cabdriver did indeed know and said he'd take my father to see him. According to the driver, if Sharif was in a good mood, he would accept my father as a visitor. But most of the time, he was in a bad mood.

Shyamal arrived at Sharif's house and knocked on the door. Imagine walking up to Jack Nicholson's mansion and asking to be let inside so that you could give him a fist bump. A man who wasn't Sharif answered and asked my father who he was, where he was from, and what he wanted. The man paused and looked Shyamal up and down. My father wondered if his gambit just might work.

"He said, 'Okay, wait. I cannot give you a guarantee.' And then he went back inside," Shyamal continued. It turned out that on this particular day Sharif *was* in a bad mood. He would not invite my father inside.

"It was a dream of my life. I only wanted to see him for a second."

My poor father. He had gone all that way for nothing. But even in rejection, Shyamal was moved. "I was very lucky," he said. "I love this man. Omar Sharif. *Doctor Zhivago* is one of the best movies of the world."

There is a part of me that wonders if the cabdriver, seeing my father's trusting naiveté, took him on a long ride to his cousin's house for the high cab fare and an amusing prank. Maybe the cabbie had no idea where Sharif lived. But I'd rather believe that Sharif peered out his window that day to see my father and that his day was brightened by Shyamal's presence, even if he wasn't feeling up to entertaining strangers.

I also wondered, after Shyamal finished telling the story, whether he had become delusional before leaving the United States, and that's why the doctors told him he shouldn't travel for a bit. In this scenario, some sort of grandiose sense of confidence pushed him to stroll up to Sharif's front door.

But my biggest takeaway was the surprise of learning my father was *that* sick when he left the country; that he was too ill to even get on a plane. In his first email to me after arriving in India in 2007, he had said he was too sick to live in New Jersey by himself, which sounded like nonsense and just added to my confusion and anger. Hearing the Sharif story helped me understand. The premise underlying the story is that he was unable to even get on a plane for so long that he found the free time to track down Sharif. More than a surprising tale about one man's quest to meet his idol, Shyamal's story made me realize that his illness hadn't just been a weak excuse for him to abandon his kids. It was real.

As Shyamal finished his story, I decided I wasn't yet ready to ask what he meant by being sick.

We walked back to the living room, where there were several paintings hanging on Shyamal's walls that he was excited to show us. My father, besides being a tennis player, a cosmologist, and a celebrity spotter, was also an art collector. Not just any kind of collector, though. These were specifically commissioned paintings, indicative of his obsession with history. By his estimation, a lot of historical paintings were incorrect. He told us that he had an artist deliver paintings that, in his eyes, were more historically accurate.

In a phrase, he was fact-checking famous paintings.

One was Shyamal's take on *The Duke of Wellington at Waterloo,* originally by the British artist Robert Alexander Hillingford, depicting the Belgium battle that ended Napoleon's empire.

Hillingford's version shows the duke triumphantly on his horse in the center of the frame, trying to rally his troops in the midst of battle. In the lower right of the painting, there is a kneeling soldier with white hair.

"Who would send this old man to a battlefield?" Shyamal said incredulously. "So I changed his hair."

The white-haired man was probably just wearing a powdered wig, but Shyamal had said it took eight months to have this painting completed. I didn't want to ruin it for him. Additionally, he felt that the painting didn't have enough dead bodies around the duke, since Wellington was giving his speech in the middle of the battle. So he added more casualties of war. In Shyamal's version, there is a snare drum on the grass by the duke's feet, left by a poor drummer who lost his life to Shyamal's fact-checking.

This was nothing compared to Shyamal's version of *The Last Supper*—yes, the da Vinci piece.

"We did a lot of research," Shyamal said, adding, "I did not like certain things about the painting. I have full respect for Leonardo da Vinci." I was picturing my father at home stewing about da Vinci and angrily calling an artist to say, "Get me the RIGHT version of *The Last Supper*! Not that there's anything wrong with da Vinci!"

Shyamal told us that around the time of the Last Supper, Jesus and his apostles were in hiding. Because of that, my father felt that wherever they were eating wouldn't have a fancy tablecloth, like the one Shyamal said that da Vinci painted in his version. So he had the artist change the tablecloth to a simpler white one.

Shyamal knew the story about Jesus washing the feet of his disciples at the Last Supper, an indication of humility.

"After cleaning of the feet by Jesus Christ," Shyamal said, "nobody would wear sandals. I wouldn't allow it! No matter what the truth is!" The apostles in Shyamal's *The Last Supper* are all barefoot.

Thank goodness Shyamal didn't live in Jordan. At the end of 2018, journalists at a publication called *Al Wakeel News* posted a version of *The Last Supper* with Salt Bae, the Turkish celebrity chef who is best known for creatively seasoning meat, into the background. The Jordanian government arrested the journalists responsible.

I had a great laugh about Shyamal's peculiarities when we got back to the hotel that night, particularly his saying "No matter what the truth is!" This is the exact kind of shit I do—pointing out plot holes in movies, television shows, and plays. It is unbearable to binge watch anything with me. I nitpick it all. I still don't get why Buzz Lightyear froze when adults walked into the room in *Toy Story* if he didn't know he was a toy. Don't get me started on any movie involving time travel.

Maybe Shyamal and I were both more alike than I realized. Maybe I'm a nitpicking asshole about art because of him. And, more frighteningly, after what he told me about Belur Math: Maybe I have my comedic sense because of him.

Yikes.

We all had dinner at the flat, which consisted of a fish curry and potatoes. Suparna was an excellent cook. Out of tiredness, we munched in silence.

After dinner, we said goodbye to Susmita, and Shyamal had a driver take us back to our hotel.

Shyamal and I had spent the day together. I was thirty, and we'd never done that before. It was a nice day, but a little bit like being thrown into the deep end of the pool.

In the car, I stared blankly out the window. The constant honking of cars had become white noise now. I wasn't processing the sights or much of anything at all on the car ride back.

"If we had never come, and you had found out about all of

these parts of him after he had passed away, I think it would have been so bad," Wesley turned to me and said.

"Yeah."

I didn't have much to say.

"One thing I kept thinking about today when we were driving around is: What if you had been born here? What would your life have been like?" Wesley said.

"Yeah."

"You wouldn't be you."

"I wouldn't be me," I repeated in a low monotone.

"I never would have known you."

"Never would have known me."

I looked out the window, hearing but not registering what Wesley was saying.

"It's just your circumstances: You were born in the United States because your dad was an engineer and all of those things. But for any of us, it's circumstances," Wesley said. "You could have been someone else."

SEVEN

"Do you wish you were closer?"

Shyamal's apartment had a small sunroom off the living room filled with an array of potted plants, with other greenery peering in through floor-to-ceiling windows, not unlike the porch at Bishakha's. Shyamal's had a livelier view, though. There was the constant stream of tuk-tuks, cyclists, and foot traffic, but the pitter-patter of the rain against the windows made it sound almost peaceful.

I spent some time immersed in the view from the second story before sitting down at the kitchen table. The white woven tablecloth was carefully covered with a protective layer of plastic, and there were plastic floral placemats on top of that. Freshly washed water glasses had been placed in front of each seat, upside down, waiting for our next meal. Wesley sat at the far end of the table, Shyamal at the other. I was in the middle. The room's primary light fixture flickered on and off, plunging the flat into and out of the dark, a harbinger of the conversation about to occur.

I placed a voice recorder between my father and me. *Beep.* A red light flicked on as I pressed the circular button in the center.

Shyamal hunched over the table with his hands placed apart, palms down. I sat up straight, put my elbows on the surface, and interlocked my hands in front of my face. We were both wearing dark blue T-shirts.

It was our second full day in Kolkata, but it felt like we had been there much longer. Over the next two days, interrupted only by visits to his brothers, I probed my father and asked him everything I didn't know about him. I began the conversation impassively and inquisitive, with my journalistic instincts fully engaged, which may be odd for a child asking a parent questions.

This trip had so far resulted in our first ever shared beer. Our first time touring a city together. Our first car ride in more than a decade. That was the fun stuff.

This would, however, be a new type of first. Our kitchen table talks were frank and, at times, hurtful. I had come this far. I had to find out who he really was. And maybe—just maybe—it would shed light into who I am.

After I hit the RECORD button, I remarked to Shyamal, "This is for the book I'm writing."

"You're writing a book on India?" Shyamal asked. I told him no. Keep in mind, here, my answer to him was a source of much amusement and frustration. I had told Shyamal several times before the trip that I was doing a book about our family. I told him again during the interview. And immediately afterward. And when we got back to the United States. And in the following month. And each time, he'd remark, "You're writing a book on India?" I'd have to correct him each time. I wasn't writing some grand anthropological treatise on a modernizing, diverse democracy. I was writing about us.

I started with the basics: "When were you born?"

Yes, it was simple, but beyond an approximate guess, I didn't know his age. My father leaned over the table to put his mouth closer to the recorder.

"My actual year of birth is July 1943," Shyamal said, but he didn't know what day.

"You don't know your birthday?" I asked.

"I know my official birthday, which is January 31, 1945," Shyamal said.

I thought he might have been messing with me. It's what I would have done with a ridiculous question if I were him. But I played along: Why did he have two different birth dates?

"Those days, things were different because parents were supposed to keep the age a little lower so they would have more time to look for a job," Shyamal said. "Yes, it is customary to do a year or year and a half. Why? Because for every job or admission to schools and colleges, there is an age limit. So to put the child in an advantageous situation, they reduced the age. And there were no birth certificates at the time."

So officially on his documentation, my father was seventy-three years old. But in reality, he was about to turn seventy-five. And it was common, according to Shyamal, for parents to deflate their children's ages for their advancement. It makes sense if you think about it: You'd rather be known as a wunderkind than normal in comparison to your peers.

My father traced the birth year of his father, Sachindra Kumar Deb, to about 1889 or 1890, in Sylhet, a prosperous district known for its tea gardens. It was in a region that would come to be known as Bangladesh, and this is where Shyamal grew up. He moved to Kolkata as a young adult.

If I may, here is a brief and possibly confusing history lesson: In 1947, the British ended their colonial rule over India and implemented the Partition, creating the territories of India and

Pakistan. Pakistan, although constitutionally one nation-state, was geographically separated into West Pakistan and East Pakistan. The provinces of Bengal and Assam were reconstituted as three new provinces: West Bengal and Assam (without Sylhet) in India, and East Bengal, which, in 1956, changed its official name to East Pakistan. The district of Sylhet was singled out, and its fate was to be decided by a referendum. The referendum resulted in most of Sylhet becoming part of East Pakistan. So Shyamal, having been born before the Partition, was technically born in British India, in the province of Assam, and he'd grown up in East Pakistan.

In 1971, East Pakistan splintered and became Bangladesh, after a civil war had broken out between both provinces of Pakistan. So when my father moved to Kolkata in 1959 to attend engineering school, Bangladesh hadn't yet been created. After Bangladesh was established, the Deb family members began migrating to India, except for my grandparents and a few uncles, who remained behind.

Education was of paramount importance to my grandfather. It was difficult to attain a satisfactory education when he was growing up—"a rare situation," as Shyamal put it. My father said Sachindra still managed to get his law degree and went on to become a successful defense attorney. He was well known in the district, and he pushed for all of his children to become educated as well. Shyamal himself had two private tutors all the way through college.

"Were you close with him?" I asked Shyamal.

"No," he answered bluntly. "I'm being honest with you. No."

During the conversation, whenever Shyamal tried to recall a memory, he would push down with his hands and tilt his head upward and his mouth into a slight frown, as if he was searching the clouds for an answer. Other times, he'd clench his fists, like he was a Heinz ketchup bottle and someone was trying to squeeze the last drop out of him. I, on the other hand, sat there frozen and expressionless. I was Lester Holt conducting an interview in prime time, throwing in the occasional nod of understanding. To an outsider, this may have seemed like I saw this as a clinical exercise.

"Why?" I asked.

"Age difference," Shyamal said. "The role of the father was different in those days. Everybody was afraid of the father. Mother was the one who raised us."

My grandmother's name was Binodini.

"Were you afraid of your father?" I pressed.

Shyamal's reaction to my question almost made me jump.

"OH YESSSSSSSSSS! OF COURSE!" he exclaimed. We had been together for a couple of days and I still wasn't used to the sudden crescendo of his voice. As Shyamal talked, his eyes widened through his glasses, which seemed to take up half his face. His hand gestures increased. He reminded me of someone acting out Shakespeare at their first audition. I worried that he might, in his excitement, knock over one of the glasses on the table.

"It was not like this relationship," he continued, beckoning to me. "All of us were afraid of my father, very afraid. He used to love us a lot."

He added: "But you used to avoid him. Because he used to stop our freedom, our movement. Discipline us."

It was not like this relationship.

There was such a cognitive dissonance here. Shyamal said he was afraid of Sachindra and that they were not close. He then said this was different from his relationship with me. Meanwhile, I would say about my father what he said about his: We weren't close, and I used to avoid him. I was never *afraid* of him, and he wasn't the disciplinarian. But then again, he was barely on my radar.

Then there was the matter of his siblings. Shyamal said he wasn't close to them either.

"I was special, and let me tell you something about it: I was different than any of them. I had talents from a young age," Shyamal said.

"What kind of talents?" I asked.

"People say I was a good-looking kid. I don't know that. Everybody says that," Shyamal said. I let out a belly laugh. This is the kind of thing Donald Trump would say: *Many people tell me that I have the best smile. The biggest smile. I'm not going to say it. The polls say it. The polls that aren't fake, that is. Which is all of them. Except Fox.*

"I could sing well," he went on. "I acted on the stage. I was doing good at the school. So naturally I drew attraction from other people. There was not a single public function in our town where I did not perform."

A handsome, high-achieving academic who could kick it on the stage? If India had prom kings, Shyamal might've been a monarch. Shyamal said Sachindra was the one who encouraged him to pursue music. But when I asked him if his father was proud of him, Shyamal said no. "He was not proud, but he expected me to go somewhere, in the sense that I'll reach some position," Shyamal said. "I'm not average. I'm much above average. He knew that."

I'm much above average. Goodness, that would have been a great yearbook quote.

My grandfather was also active in local politics, Shyamal said. Sachindra advised the Pakistani government on issues such as education, even playing an instrumental role in saving a local school from being closed. Though Shyamal didn't say it, I imagined that he would have crowned himself prom king there too.

Sachindra was roughly seventy-three years old when he passed away in 1962. Shyamal found out about the death through a telegram. Officially, he was seventeen at the time. But in reality, he was nineteen. He wasn't keen on discussing his father's death, only saying that it was of "old age."

"When he died, his body was being taken for cremation," Shyamal said. "Hindu representative, Muslim representative, Christian representative—they all held his body on their shoulders for a long procession. He helped people so much free of charge. Hindus. Muslims. Christians. Everybody treated him as a second god."

"Do you wish you were closer with him?" I asked. It was a reasonable question, given how laudatory Shyamal was toward his father.

"No," Shyamal said, without skipping a beat. "I have a different personality, believe me. I will not hesitate to say that I think I have some superiority complex."

At least he was self-aware. He said this stemmed from being the son of a well-known community figure. As an example, he cited being a goalie when he played soccer. Sometimes his team would win needing very little from him, yet it was his name that was listed at the top in postgame accolades. He excelled in school and would routinely hear comments like, "He's Sachindra Deb's son! Of course he'll be first!" He was used to receiving attention, even more so than his siblings. It went to his head, he admitted.

"Did you feel your father knew you beyond your professional accomplishments? Do you feel he knew you personally?" I asked. Shyamal didn't understand the question at first. He shook his head. The age difference played a role, he noted. Sachindra was almost fifty-five years old when Shyamal was born.

"He had very high expectations for me," Shyamal said, still not comprehending what I meant. It was like asking a goldfish if it likes cheeseburgers.

I told him that there's a professional side of us as humans and a personal side. "I'm a *New York Times* reporter, and then I have a personal side," I said. "I like music and I like watching sports, you know, there are things that interest me outside of my résumé. Did he only view you in terms of how good your résumé was?"

"He never looked at his children like that," Shyamal said. "In those days, father means protecting the family, give them best education, raise them the best you can. That's it. Those concepts are gone. Even in our time, when I was your age, much younger, we grew up under the shadow of the guardian."

Shyamal said that his father told him to go to engineering school, so he went to engineering school. Every decision ran through Sachindra before he died.

"What if you didn't want to be an engineer? You're a musical person. What if you wanted to do that professionally? What would your father have said?" I asked.

"Good question you ask," Shyamal said. "I wanted to always become an accordion player and work in the movie industry. That is my passion, besides the accordion. I didn't have the guts to open my mouth. I had to go to engineering, that's it. Father says, 'Go to engineering if you qualify.'"

I persisted: But what if you did open your mouth?

"No. You have to understand: You are only a sixteen-year-old kid, out of the question," Shyamal said. "It was all what they say. So when my father passed away, my eldest brother, he became the guardian. He used to tell us, 'Do this, do this, do this.'"

He was referring to Sudhirendra. After Sachindra's death, Sudhirendra, as the oldest brother, became the patriarch of the family. He was an engineer by trade. In a culture where the patriarch holds much sway over what you do and what you do not do, Shyamal said Sudhirendra was a source of resentment for him. He was a dominant figure and hard on my father.

"He was a very brilliant man," Shyamal said of Sudhirendra, who was separated by almost two decades from Shyamal. Or as my father put it: "Two decades by age, five decades by culture. Don't tell anyone."

Shyamal poking fun at someone else for not being plugged in was high comedy. Nevertheless, when my father first moved to Kolkata in 1959, he lived with Sudhirendra, who had already been living there. Shyamal told me I had met his oldest brother when he visited the United States when I was very young, but I had no recollection of this.

"Were you close growing up?" I said.

"No! Never!" Shyamal said.

"So he's not an influential figure in your life?" I said. I was surprised at his honest answer.

"The MOST INFLUENTIAL figure in my life!" Shyamal said, raising his voice and continuing. "He's North Pole. I'm South Pole in every aspect."

It's funny he said that because I sometimes think that about Sattik and me (though not in a negative way). The age difference, Shyamal added, was a big deal.

I asked him whether it bothered him that he wasn't close with his brother.

"Maybe every second," Shyamal said.

It was remarkable: Shyamal had the same regrets about Sudhirendra that I had about Shyamal.

"Close" in this context is an interesting word. Sudhirendra lived in "close" physical proximity to Shyamal, and Shyamal told me he saw him often. My father was helping to take care of his oldest brother as his health worsened. I even heard him set up a doctor's appointment for Sudhirendra. But still they weren't *close* in the way I thought of the word. I've always thought of the concept of closeness as being comfortable, emotionally in tune and familiar with the other person, able to read their mind like your own. But my father and Sudhirendra didn't talk about feelings. To a stranger, they would still seem close because Shyamal was taking care of Sudhirendra. It was clear to me that Shyamal did so out of a blood obligation.

"Let me tell you something," Shyamal said. "Someday I'm going to die, and I'll tell someone to read to my dear son: *Once somebody grows up, human beings don't change.* Once my boss said to me: 'He can change his dresses. He can change his shoes. He can change his glasses, but his personality doesn't change. A human being does not change.' And he was right. Everything I like, he hates; everything he likes, I hate. That's the way it is."

He was being pessimistic, and I wasn't sure I agreed with him. Maybe a person doesn't fundamentally evolve. Maybe once you reach adulthood, your cap for how much of your personality traits you can reasonably address is lower. But maturation is a form of change, and it's why I was sitting adjacent to him at that moment, rather than an ocean's distance apart.

"But you don't have to like the same things," I said. "Did you guys clash growing up?"

"Not face-to-face. We did not have the guts to do that," Shyamal said. "But in my mind, yes."

I wondered: Sudhirendra was ninety-two and close to the end of his life. Did he still define his relationship with Shyamal as being the elder?

"He is not only elder. He is the commander in chief," Shyamal answered.

"He doesn't have many years left," I said. "If you're not close with him, is that something you think about at all?"

I was pressing on this because I was still giving in to my instincts as a reporter: I wanted to dig deeper. But I was also indirectly letting my own thoughts about my connection with my parents seep into the conversation. My father said he wished his bond with Sudhirendra was "much better" and that it was "not even in the acceptable range."

"No, no, no! My relationship with him is purely mechanical," Shyamal said. "Let me give you an example. When you landed at the airport the day before yesterday, the moment I saw Wesley, I became so thrilled. A great thrill. I had an affection for her then and there. I never saw her before. She was there for one minute and I was so thrilled by it. Why? Do you know how much I love you? Ultimately, it's connected."

I wasn't quite sure what he meant by "connected" or the word "mechanical." He clarified: "Your relationship with the driver—purely mechanical. Your relationship with the hotel manager, it's mechanical. No emotion involved at this moment."

Ah. He meant "obligatory" or, read another way, "transactional."

"But the driver is not my brother," I countered.

"What is a brother? What is a sister? What is a relationship? You're my son. How long have we been disconnected physically? Eleven years," Shyamal said.

At the time, I really had no idea what he meant by this and was a bit frustrated. We had to leave to go meet Sudhirendra, so the conversation ended for the day. Shyamal wasn't ready to divulge more.

All I could get out of him was this: "A certain turning moment of my life was drastically influenced by his order. By his order. It affected my life seriously." He added, "So I hated him. It's the same—I listened to him because of the fact that he's the one who helped me to go to my education."

Shyamal clearly felt wounded by Sudhirendra. But I was

struck that he still felt a duty to his eldest brother: to help take care of him in his old age, even while resenting the transactional nature of their relationship.

I had never even thought about Shyamal in those terms. What if one year ago Shyamal had fallen seriously ill? Would I have flown to India to help nurse my father back to health? In the way Susmita had for Sudhirendra, her father-in-law? What about Bishakha? She lives within driving distance of New York. Would I go to her at a moment's notice, the way Shyamal did for Sudhirendra?

The conversation ended, but as we prepared to leave for Sudhirendra's house, Shyamal asked a question I didn't expect.

"Did we disconnect our relationship ever?" Shyamal said.

The word "relationship" was doing heavy lifting here. It's hard to disconnect from something that I felt barely existed.

I said, "Well, let's talk about that—"

But Shyamal cut me off with a soliloquy.

"Maybe from your side," Shyamal said. "My side, no. No. I always loved my son. I always look at your picture, remember how he's doing. So did I with Sattik."

He continued, "Relationships are very much emotionally guided. Relationships between siblings, parents, children: emotion. No matter where it is, they're our parents. They're our fathers. They're our children. But the degree varies on the relationship. Other types are mechanical. Other types are professional. It's very difficult to define a relationship quantitatively."

I was stuck, though, on his suggesting that *I* was solely responsible for our disconnecting. I could feel my blood starting to simmer, my journalistic veneer melting away. It wasn't as if I woke up one morning and decided I didn't want a relationship with my father. Lest we forget, *he* was the one who left the country without warning.

We were running late and were teetering on the edge of a conversation for which I didn't yet have the energy. I had an uncle to meet.

EIGHT

"I might not be around."

Here is an internal conversation I recently had with myself:

Do I want to get married? Yes.

Do I want it to be Star Trek*–themed?* Yes.

Will it actually be? Well—

Will there be a band? Yes, what are the Gin Blossoms up to?

What will be my wedding song? "All I've Ever Known" from the *Hadestown* Broadway soundtrack. But about the *Star Trek*—

What about the color scheme? Green, like the Orions in *Star Trek*.

It's never going to happen. That's rude. Who even are you?

I am you. Good point.

Nobody wants to attend a Star Trek*–themed wedding. Including your fiancée.* Shut up.

What about a Garfield *theme instead?* Who are you again?

I am you. Right.

Garfield? I'm intrigued.

Hear me out. You serve lasagna and do it on a Monday. Wow, yes.

I am you. You are me. We're doing it.

This me-on-me conversation is probably why Michelle broke up with me after college. She saw the future. And she wanted to get married on a Saturday.

I have put a lot of thought into what I want out of a wedding, especially in recent years. I'm at the age where it's more likely that I attend a wedding on a weekend than go for a jog. Also, the jogs are more painful.

I started picturing my wedding when I was in middle school. For one thing, I would see weddings quite a bit on television. Any one of my favorite shows—*The West Wing, Star Trek: Deep Space Nine, WWF SmackDown!, Sesame Street, The Sopranos,* you name it—had wedding episodes. More important, they had viewers like me to watch them.

Most of these weddings seemed *so happy.* It was as if there was an unwritten television law forbidding families from fighting in the presence of a soon-to-be married couple. Watching these scenes in conjunction with my family's history instilled a desire in me to have a wife and kids and not have the relationship with them that my parents had with each other and me. This in itself is not unhealthy. What *is* unhealthy is the way it started manifesting itself in my dating life: When I would get too clingy and marriage-oriented too early on.

The dream wedding itself has gone through various iterations in my mind throughout the decades. At first, because I was in middle school, I was totally on board with a theme wedding. After all, so many of my classmates had elementary school birthday parties at Chuck E. Cheese. I figured weddings were the same thing. Also, Will and Lisa had one in *Fresh Prince of Bel-Air.*

In high school, my vision changed after my parents' divorce. A lavish ceremony celebrating nuptials became unattractive. I knew for sure I didn't want a traditional Indian ceremony. And what if my marriage ended up the way my parents' did? You'd have all those toasters to return. Instead, I pictured a quiet ceremony. My fiancée and me, walking down the aisle to Dave Matthews playing "Crash into Me."

Sattik got married my sophomore year of college. It was my first time attending a wedding of someone with whom I had a personal relationship. All the past ceremonies I had been to were for friends of my parents. My brother's wedding was going to be my first up-close experience with the vision I had for my own life.

He had met Erica, an outgoing and caring woman from Toms River, a nearby New Jersey suburb, a few years prior. I was happy for him. It felt like a jailbreak for my brother, an opportunity for him to outwardly give and receive something with which we had little experience: healthy, unconditional love. I was nineteen at the time, and he asked me to be his best man. With all the television shows I watched growing up, I felt prepared. Although it was a bit difficult to plan a bachelor party, since Sattik didn't drink and I was only nineteen. This wasn't going to be *American Pie.*

We planned a night out in Manhattan with a few of his friends: dinner in Little Italy, followed by a show at Gotham

Comedy Club, one of the city's biggest stand-up venues. It wasn't exactly a romp in Las Vegas, but it was very much suited to Sattik, which is what matters after all. (Sattik, if he ever has to return the favor and plan my bachelor party, is in for it, since I'd like mine to be in space.)

We are very different people. He was a quiet nerd in high school and college, whereas I've always had a boisterous side. Sattik's work ethic is unmatched. He puts the same effort into changing the light bulb that he does into his career. Me? Let's put it this way: How many Sopans does it take to screw in that light bulb? It depends on how distracted the Sopans are by the balloon that just flew by the window.

Growing up, Sattik filled some of that father-figure gap when he could. He was my hero. Until he moved out, he made sure I was cared for when my parents weren't parenting. I played catch with him. He taught me the importance of Billy Joel's contributions to the American cultural catalog. He was also a disciplinarian. One summer when I was in elementary school, Sattik grounded me and made me write lines for an entire month, just like Bishakha would, because he caught me watching *Judge Judy*. What can I say? I had strong feelings about the judicial system, whereas he wanted to *be* the judicial system. Other times, he'd make me do push-ups as a form of punishment. I got the last laugh, though. Sattik is a results-oriented guy, and, well, my arms remained twigs.

My brother didn't really care what kind of wedding he had. Erica wanted a traditional Christian ceremony, and Sattik, in his good judgment, was willing to do whatever his bride-to-be wanted. They picked a church on the campus of Rutgers University, where they both went to school.

Shyamal wasn't at the ceremony, which lasted roughly an hour, because he had left for India by this point and my brother had had his own rift with him. There was, however, a brown side of the aisle, featuring my mother, my uncle Atish, his wife, Sima, and their son, Sagnik, who is a few years younger than me; and a white side of the aisle, where Erica's family sat. It wasn't intentionally segregated, mind you, nor was this a big deal. It was still an unintentionally amusing visual.

And the thing about this Christian wedding: My family had never been to church before. They didn't know what to do. They knew *Sister Act*. I think they were expecting a gospel service. And they were used to Indian weddings, which are a slightly tamer version of Burning Man. If Indian ceremonies are Burning Man, Christian weddings are a night at the New York Philharmonic. The brown side of the aisle didn't know when to sit, stand, or sing hymns. And they were wondering when the action would take off. *Where was the fire? Where are the appetizers? How come everybody showed up on time?* It was like how I feel watching a Wes Anderson film: *This is beautiful. Looks amazing. When does this thing get going? Oh. It's over. Huh.*

As I was standing on the dais, I thought to myself: *This is not what I want.* Getting married in a church without being religious myself didn't seem authentic, no matter who my fiancée is. Not that I wanted Burning Man either. Frankly, I wanted Chuck E. Cheese.

In the lead-up to the ceremony, Bishakha took me aside and sternly said, "Shambo, I want you to have an Indian wedding." I half expected her to follow that up with, "That's an order, Lieutenant." I didn't take it seriously. We were distant at this point. I had thought a lot about my dream wedding and I knew that wasn't it. Why lie to the many Hindu gods about my commitment to the cause?

Now I'm not so sure I need a wedding at all. A party is fine. Or nothing. A life partner is cool with me too. Except when I got to India, it wasn't totally left up to me. Some family members wanted to speed up the process, whether we wanted to or not.

Sudhirendra's house was a fifteen-minute drive from Shyamal's flat. It was one of the rare treks through Kolkata during which the streets weren't packed with cars. I snapped pictures out my passenger-side window with a DSLR camera I had brought with me on the trip. For the first time, I noticed the amount of lush greenery complementing the quaint little shops cramming the sidewalks. Some of the towering tree branches hovering over the street looked like they were emerging from the buildings themselves.

"The last few days have been so hot. I was concerned," Shyamal said, from the front of the car. He didn't have to shout for once. "Today, at least, it is a little mild." It was a minimum ninety degrees and humid outside.

Sudhirendra's wife, Namita, was there to greet us, along with my cousin Susmita. She offered us tea. Minutes later, Sudhirendra shuffled in with the help of a cane and we all settled into chairs in the cozy living room with light blue walls and a shuttered window that barely filtered the streaming light. My father's eldest sibling couldn't speak much—"perhaps old age," as Shyamal might have said. But he was an imposing figure, six feet tall and with more hair than I had. Judging from the way the energy in the room shifted toward him when he walked in, my father's description of him as the one-time patriarch of the family hit home.

I would do the lion's share of conversing, mostly in Bengali, while Wesley sat nearby not understanding a word. But every now and then Sudhirendra would beckon me over to mutter one phrase repeatedly in English: "You should go visit Japan."

There was no explanation. No one else in the room heard his

suggestion. *"You should go to Japan."* I didn't know if this was genuine advice, code for a hidden treasure, or a signal that he was being held against his will. What could I say? I told him we would go someday.

Sudhirendra asked if I recalled his visit from my childhood.

"I remember a little bit," I lied.

"You can speak Bengali also?" Sudhirendra said.

"He can speak clean Bengali," Shyamal chimed in. "Wesley graduated from Harvard Law School."

Sudhirendra couldn't hear well.

"Harvard! *HARVARD GRADUATE!*" Shyamal said, this time louder.

My aunt looked at Wesley and said in Bengali, *"Bishon mishti."* ("She's very sweet.")

But Namita was drowned out because my father was still saying, "Harvard! *Harvard!"*

"Kamon aacho, Dadhu?" I said to Sudhirendra, which translates to "How are you?" *Dadhu* typically refers to an elder.

"I am the age of ninety-two," Sudhirendra said. "I have lots of complaints. When did you learn to speak Bengali?"

"I've been speaking it since I was little," I said, slowly and deliberately.

"He can sing too!" Shyamal added. I can't, of course. Not really. But we didn't need to get bogged down in petty details like that.

"Really, though, I don't speak it much anymore. But here, I've been speaking it again," I said. My aunt concurred with Sudhirendra that my Bengali was top-notch. I kept trying to translate on the fly for Wesley, but she stopped me and said, "Don't worry about me."

When the conversation found a lull, Sudhirendra threw in another, *"Go visit Japan!"* for good measure.

After about an hour, my aunt called Wesley and me into another room, which I assumed meant we were getting the tour of the place.

Instead, Namita gathered us in a corner next to a makeshift shrine, placed on a dresser covered in pieces of red silk cloth and featuring several religious emblems. There were multiple silver plates with flowers on them, along with framed pictures, across from a bed with a green sheet neatly enveloping it. Another striking window perpendicular to the shrine filled the room with light from outside.

I pointed at one of the emblems I recognized.

"That's Ganesha?" I said, remembering the Hindu deity with an elephant head.

"You forgot *Ganesha*?" my aunt said.

I hadn't. Forgetting Ganesha—one of the most worshipped gods in Hinduism—would be like a Christian not remembering Jesus Christ. There was also a picture of Ramakrishna, the influential Indian spiritual leader from the 1800s.

Wordlessly, Namita arranged for Wesley and me to face the shrine at the foot of the bed. I had a brief second of panic, afraid that perhaps my aunt was about to request that we say a prayer. I wasn't prepared for that. The gods up there weren't prepared for that. I'd need an instruction manual of some sort.

The room itself was of a moderate size, and as I turned toward the door, I noticed Shyamal and Susmita observing the proceedings with some bemusement.

My aunt revealed her true intentions: This was an *ashirwad*, she said.

I had to plumb the depths of my memories to recall what that was. The word sounded familiar, but I couldn't put my finger on where I'd heard it.

Of course: a blessing ceremony.

I remembered because my mother had thrown one for Sattik and Erica before they officially got married. It was Sattik's way of throwing Bishakha a bone since they planned on a Christian wedding. How it worked was that family and friends lined up in front of the seated couple to touch their foreheads with a mixture of rice and grass blades. It is usually reserved for engaged or married couples and signifies a family's acceptance of the bride and groom by the elders. Wesley and I were not engaged, not that it made a difference in Namita's eyes.

"Take this," my aunt said.

She had Wesley and me clasp our hands and hold some of the pieces she picked up off the shrine. She followed up by wrapping one of the red cloths around our hands and whispering a quick blessing. Then my aunt pinched each of our cheeks and turned to my waiting father and Susmita, who were eagerly snapping pictures.

"When they come here again next time, I might not be around," Namita said. "So I gave them this." In English, she added: "Souvenirs!"

The amazing thing about this is that Wesley had *no idea* what was going on because my aunt spoke the whole time in Bengali. Everything happened so fast that I didn't have a chance to explain it to her. I was having trouble keeping up. In the pictures my father and Susmita took, Wesley looks like a hostage. All she knew was that we were suddenly in another room, with cloth being wrapped around our hands and pictures being taken of us. If she had doubts about marrying me sometime in the future, she had to keep them suppressed. As far as my aunt and uncle were concerned, Wesley and I were married.

After the ceremony, we said our goodbyes. Namita gave us the pieces we'd clasped in our hands to take home with us. Wesley and I touched the feet of my aunt and uncle as a show of respect before we climbed into the car. I told Wesley we would have to go to Japan at some point. We were quasi-married now anyway, I told her, so another hop across the world seemed like a normal step. And while the *ashirwad* wasn't the Chuck E. Cheese ceremony I pictured, and Dave Matthews was nowhere to be found, I felt strangely comfortable with what Namita had put us through. *It was odd,* I thought. *Usually, I find rituals like that excruciating.* But for this one, I had Wesley with me. And even after realizing what had just taken place, she was comfortable too. And maybe that's all I needed.

Around the time I first started writing material for stand-up, I wrote this joke:

> *Lots of people complain about having to do online dating. They say it's forced, inorganic matchmaking for the eventual purpose of procreation. You know what my parents called that? The good old days.*

It was one of those cracks with a false premise: Of course, I didn't think my parents would have called them the good old days, given how their marriage turned out.

I've always been baffled by the concept of arranged marriage. I spent many hours in my first couple of years writing comedy trying to come up with material on the topic. I didn't get very far, in part, because it's a very cliché thing for brown comics to joke about. But, more important, nothing ever came to me. At least I had nothing funny to say, perhaps owing to my negative experience, and nothing interesting to tell audiences that they hadn't heard already.

This was why I found my next conversation with Susmita simultaneously perplexing and illuminating. For my cousin, arranged marriage not only made sense, it worked—the result of which was a stable, well-adjusted American family.

After seeing Sudhirendra and Namita, we went back to Shyamal's flat. Susmita came with us to spend the rest of the afternoon. In the living room, we talked about her husband, Somnath, whom she married in India. The marriage hadn't been fully arranged. She called it a "setup" initiated by Namita. Susmita said if she didn't want to get arranged, she didn't have to, but she was introduced to Somnath after several months of meeting potential husbands.

"How soon after you met did you get married?" I asked.

"Two weeks," Susmita said. My eyes widened. Susmita burst out laughing.

"Literally, the ceremony was two weeks later?" I said. This is how things were done almost three decades ago in India. Susmita added that she had Indian friends who are both PhDs in the United States who saw each other for the first time on their wedding day.

I looked at Wesley and said, "We are way behind. Their courtship was shorter than our trip to India." Then I turned back to Susmita, who said that during those two weeks, she met Somnath's family first. Eventually, the two of them went out for dinner to begin getting to know each other as best as they could in two weeks.

Shyamal, who was only half listening to the conversation, interjected: "It is a tradition in India, like fifty years back, that once the marriage is done, you have a child in a year or in eighteen months. Why? Because with more time, then you find out each other's negative points."

He noticed the horrified look on my face.

"Yes! That's the way things worked," Shyamal went on. "But once the child is born, the focus goes toward the child; you can forgive and forget the other. Dating for five years? You'll never be together for fifty years."

To have a child to try to mask the deficiencies in a relationship seemed like a recipe for disaster. I wondered if this was why my parents had Sattik and me. It was a question for later.

Through other setups arranged by Susmita's mother, she had previously met other potential suitors, but Somnath, in her words, was "the final pick."

"So you had turned down other people?" I said.

"It was the other way for me," Susmita said. She initially turned him down too.

"I would rather go with the other one," Susmita said she told her father.

But he convinced her to marry Somnath.

Wesley jumped in: "So it's a period of several months, where you're meeting a bunch of people and then it was down to two, and you wanted to go with the other one, and he said, 'No, no'?"

"Yes! Wesley, I'm very impressed," Susmita said.

And you know what? It worked. Susmita's father told her to trust him. She did. They were happily married, and they remain so. Susmita and Somnath have raised two lovely children. Their son, Ron, was managing a state representative campaign in Connecticut at the time. Both Ron and their daughter, Trisha, were about to graduate from the University of Connecticut. Susmita, Somnath, Ron, and Trisha had the last name Deb, just like me. But they are the happy version of our story, a realization of the American Dream my parents knew nothing about.

That afternoon, we went to Belur Math, the temple complex on the Ganges. At night, Shyamal wanted us to indulge his interest in the cosmos. He took us to the Birla Planetarium for a showing of a film narrated by Robert Redford about cosmic collisions, a film for which he couldn't stop expressing his excitement. The planetarium was cylindrical and dome-shaped, with two visible pillars on the outside, a bit like the Jefferson Memorial in Washington, D.C. Several fountains on a gated greenery spouted water outside the building.

The line to purchase tickets stretched from the ticket booth to the street, about a quarter of a mile. The occasional stray dog navigated the grounds. This was a popular attraction, it seemed, but the line didn't deter my father. After gaining admission, ushers helped us find seats inside the theater.

Maybe I was still jetlagged. Or maybe Redford's voice was too soothing for the film's own good. There was also the reclining chairs and air-conditioning. But I fell asleep during the film. I was out like a light. Okay, in planetarium lingo, I was out like the dimmed star I'm sure Redford explained in the story. But either way, I was gone after the opening credits. I put on a show though walking out of the theater, matching Shyamal's raves about the movie.

After Birla, we went to the outskirts of the Victoria Memorial, an early 1900s marble structure built in tribute to Queen Victoria that is now a museum. We couldn't enter the grounds because it was too late at night, but Shyamal insisted that the lit-up building was worth the trip.

He was correct. It was quite a sight, even though you had to peer through the perimeter security fence and carefully manicured bushes to get a glimpse. The memorial, also featuring a dome, seemed to glow at night. It made sense why it was one of the most visited tourist sites in Kolkata. What didn't make sense was my father's method of taking photos of us as we walked on the sidewalk surrounding the memorial's grounds.

Shyamal would stop approximately every two minutes to take

shots of me and Wesley at a sliiiiiiightly different angle from the photo before. This might be normal parental behavior, but Shyamal had a point-and-shoot camera that he barely knew how to use. And he didn't know how to zoom in and out. So he pointed the lens at us, asked us to stand still, and walked back and forth until the framing in his viewscreen was what he desired. A process that should have taken five seconds took several minutes.

He would have us lean against the fence. Look at each other. Look at the building. Look at him. Have our backs turned. At one point, Wesley gave him her iPhone to take pictures with.

"Ah! This is a better camera," Shyamal said. But he kept using his, because why break with tradition?

None of these photos were going to be on the cover of *Vanity Fair.* I didn't mind, though. He was clearly having a blast. And why not enjoy the modeling gig?

No matter how long it took for him to get the shot.

NINE

"Do you follow my points?"

If Shyamal's relationship with Sudhirendra was distant, the one with his youngest brother, sixty-eight-year-old Siddhartha, was the opposite. Before we arrived at his house to meet him the next day, Shyamal called him his best friend. They are only about five years apart.

"Even now?" I asked.

"Even now," he said, without hesitation.

Siddhartha and my aunt Meera lived in a two-story flat that was also a short drive from Shyamal's. When Siddhartha greeted us, what was immediately clear is that he had a far more forceful personality than Shyamal. Don't get me wrong: Shyamal knew how to raise his voice and so apparently did Sudhirendra in his day. But Siddhartha boomed, and he spoke almost every sentence in a brusque manner. Physically, he was about the same size as Shyamal: roughly five feet and nine inches tall, average weight. His wife, shorter in stature with notably kind eyes, was much quieter.

In their living room, they inquired about our first couple of days in Kolkata. I mentioned the interactions we'd had at Belur Math, including an episode in which a crowd of children lined up to take photos with Wesley.

"Because she is sweet and beautiful," my aunt said.

"Have you heard the name of Vivekananda?" my uncle asked Wesley. He was referring to the person who established Belur Math. This would be a recurring theme of this visit. Siddhartha could speak English, but he wasn't totally fluent. So he'd ask a lot of questions. Sometimes they were rhetorical, because he wanted to make a point. Other times, it was to make sure we were listening to what he was saying, to properly understand. He'd literally say, in his abrupt cadence, "Do you follow my points? Do you follow my points? *Do. You. Follow. My. Points?!*"

"Yes, that's where—" I stepped in.

"Don't help her," Siddhartha said. "I am just arguing with her. Have you heard the name Vivekananda?"

(He meant "bantering," not arguing.)

"Well, he was telling us yesterday—" Wesley said, looking at Shyamal.

"Right, right, right. So I think you have seen the Ganges River," Siddhartha said. "Kolkata is on the bank of the Ganges. Kolkata was totally a British-ruled capital of India. Kolkata was the capital of India under the British rule, okay? So if you want to see a carbon copy of London, then you can see it in Kolkata."

Siddhartha was very observant of Indian history as well as its customs. When lunch was served, the food came in a specific order. Daal first. Then, fish with coconut wrapped in a banana leaf. Then the main course, a chicken curry. He insisted we wash our hands before the food came out, an important tenet of eating an authentic Indian dinner. I called him *kaku,* a term for "uncle."

Meera, my aunt, was *kakima*. (*Mashi* is a more general term that can also include family friends.)

"To which country do you belong?" Siddhartha asked Wesley.

"I'm American," Wesley responded.

"American, I know. But where were you born?" Siddhartha said.

"Arkansas," Wesley said.

"Bill Clinton!" Shyamal exclaimed.

"Oh, Bill Clinton!" Siddhartha echoed. "You are the daughter of the soil."

Neither of us knew what that meant in relation to the former president, but we politely laughed anyway. I spotted three portraits hanging in a row above a living room couch. When I asked Siddhartha who they were, he reacted with shock.

"First of all, you respect them. *This is my family*," Siddhartha said. He had us all stand up to look at them.

They were of my grandparents and my great-grandfather. It was the first time I had seen their faces. Siddhartha said he prayed for their blessings twice a day, once in the morning and once at night. I made a mental note here: I had seen smaller versions of these portraits on a shelf in Shyamal's flat, but tucked away among other figurines with pictures of gurus who were, presumably, not related to us.

In the center portrait was Sachindra, my grandfather, staring straight ahead. He was wearing a white shirt with buttons, thick glasses not unlike those of Buddy Holly, and his lips were pursed. There was no smile.

Sachindra's portrait was flanked on one side by my grandmother—Shyamal's mother, Binodini. Her face was angled sideways and turned toward Sachindra's painting. She was also wearing glasses, along with a white sari and headscarf. There was no smile there either. And both paintings had a dark background, which contrasted with the pink walls surrounding the frames. Later, Siddhartha told me that Somnath, Susmita's husband, was at my grandmother's bedside when she died in 1979, reading the Bhagavad Gita, the ancient Hindu text. He was a young boy at the time, but Siddhartha attributed Somnath's height—he is nearly six feet tall—to that reading.

"That's why he became so big! For the blessings! That's why I'm telling you, my friend! Collect the blessings from parents! They are more valuable than millions of dollars," Siddhartha exclaimed.

My great-grandfather's photograph was styled the same as Sachindra's, except with a light background. He had a white beard. I took a second to search his face for the resemblance to my father, since I've never seen Shyamal with facial hair.

Wesley and I delicately sat on the couch after lunch underneath the portraits as Siddhartha held court. He sat across from us, with nearly perfect posture, facing two previous generations of Debs and the next one. Shyamal hunched nearby silently listening. He eventually dozed off, occasionally jerking his head up to clarify something Siddhartha said.

"Please give me patience here, but you guys don't know about our family," my uncle said. "Secondly, I can't speak like you in English, but I'm trying."

Siddhartha came to India when he was a young boy of about twelve years old, after Sachindra died and after Shyamal had already left Sylhet.

"I myself could not dream at least forty years ago that my life would be like this," Siddhartha said. "If a guy lost his father in childhood, he lost everything. Because in our society, father is the main key. He gave the shelter. He gave the food. When father is no more, a son has no way to survive unless there is hard labor and hard struggle."

He studied chemistry and landed a job in pharmaceuticals in

1972 at age twenty-two. He was paid a hundred and fifty rupees per month. It was not enough to get by, so he put an advertisement in a newspaper offering to tutor children in the equivalent of eighth to twelfth grades. He brought in enough customers to make up to a thousand rupees a month. Siddhartha had ambitions to start a pharmaceutical company of his own. In 1980, with forty thousand rupees in his account (about six hundred dollars today), he met my *kakima*.

"It was not a love marriage. It was a social marriage," Siddhartha said, using another term for an arranged union. Meera's parents went to Siddhartha's boss at the pharmaceutical company he was working at to inquire about the young chemist.

"It was a blessing from God," Siddhartha said. They were married less than a month later.

My *kakima* sat on a chair adjacent to Siddhartha. Like Shyamal, she was silent for the conversation. Unlike him, she was awake.

"She inspired me highly," Siddhartha said. He looked at me pointedly. "Look, if you can't get inspiration from her, you can't produce."

"She inspires me daily," I repeated, rather awkwardly exchanging glances with Wesley.

In the 1980s, Siddhartha, at the urging of Meera, started the business that would make his career: He began providing the plants required for pharmaceutical medicine to several companies, making use of both his chemistry knowledge and some botany he had learned over the years.

One of the first things Siddhartha wanted to tell us about was my grandparents. Sachindra was a "well-known lawyer," whom he called a "saintlike gentleman" and "a very simple man." Binodini was a "very affectionate lady."

"My father was earning a lot of money. On the other hand . . ." Siddhartha paused and turned to Shyamal. "What word am I looking for?"

"Donation," Shyamal popped in. His eyes remained shut.

"Donation! He earned a lot of money! But he also donated a lot of money to the people. He couldn't tolerate the sufferings of any man," Siddhartha said.

Siddhartha was deliberate in choosing his words, and he continued to have Wesley and me repeat them back to him. If he wasn't asking us to follow his points, his sentences were punctuated with a stern "What did I just say?!" Perhaps aware of how little I knew about my extended family and my complex feelings toward Shyamal, Siddhartha was acting as both a Deb family historian and a pitchman for our DNA.

"We are very much sentimental," Siddhartha said. "We always shout if any injustice is happening in front of our eyes. Thirdly, all our members are very religious. All the members of our family have established themselves by hard struggle, by sacrifice. All the members of our family are educated and well cultured."

I hadn't had the chance to ask Shyamal his thoughts on religion. But when I was growing up, I had never gotten the sense it was a big deal to him. It certainly wasn't the time to tell Siddhartha about my agnosticism, or my general lack of faith in the idea of powerful deities.

"We have three sisters. Two of them have expired," Siddhartha said.

Much of the conversation was him talking, as if he was delivering a symposium called Deb 101. Wesley and I sat silently, with inscrutable stares. There was no mysterious advice about going to Japan from Siddhartha. Quite the opposite, in fact: He had plenty to say, and it was apparent that he would consider it a sign of disrespect if we didn't drink in every word.

"My sisters were remarkable, very good housewives. They loved their husbands. And they got all these things from my mother.

Understand? *Clearly?*"

We dutifully said yes. *Clearly.* I had a feeling I knew where he was going next. Siddhartha looked at Wesley.

"You guys definitely will be happy if you get married to this boy," Siddhartha said, motioning toward me. *Oh no,* I thought to myself. *More marriage blessings?*

"Because this boy, inside his body, *runs the same blood of ours.*"

I was hoping that the next sentence out of his mouth would reveal some mind-boggling secret. Something like, *"Yer a wizard, Shambo."* Or he would tell me that the Deb blood was infused with some mutation that would be the subject of the next Marvel movie. Alas, no. There was no movie franchise in my future. Instead, the conversation turned to my father.

"There may be some accidents that happen time to time in our family. We cannot resist it. Something odd. Some events like this case. It has happened. It is an accident."

"This case?" He was beckoning toward Shyamal, referring to his marriage with my mother. Shyamal sat there impassively. Siddhartha was matter-of-factly saying Shyamal was an outlier in the family. *But that's my thing! I'm the outlier!* I thought.

I asked Siddhartha if he was close with his brothers and sisters.

"I don't like to comment about that. Please excuse me. Next question," Siddhartha said, putting his hands up defensively. "Because if I answer this question, there are so many things that will come, which I don't like to discuss. Top secret of the family."

This was a rather mysterious answer to a simple question, I thought. Maybe I *was* a wizard. There were skeletons in the Deb family closet, it appeared, but I didn't press. He was a deeply serious man and I was intimidated. This wasn't an easy feat. I've interviewed powerful people, including CEOs, presidential candidates, and celebrities. And rarely do I feel unnerved. But something about Siddhartha daunted me and kept me from pushing when he didn't want to be pushed.

Instead, I asked about his reaction to his father, Sachindra, dying.

"Oh wow," Siddhartha said, angling toward the dozing Shyamal. "Your son, these questions. They're excellent."

The mood of the conversation changed ever so slightly. Siddhartha's shoulders hunched, and though he smiled a bit more, his gestures increased. Up until now, I wasn't sure if he was enjoying this conversation. However Siddhartha seemed to have been convinced of our level of investment in hearing his answers. He turned back.

"It's very difficult. When my father expired, there were only three brothers with him. The rest of the brothers were in Kolkata. Understand? I didn't know what was going on. I saw my mother crying. I said, 'Why are you crying? What is happening? What happened?'"

While my grandmother was shocked by the death, Siddhartha wasn't. Sachindra had told him about it before it happened. He prophesied it, from Siddhartha's telling.

"My father knew his time of expiration," Siddhartha said. "Can you imagine it? My father knew. He told me at least two years before. 'You are my youngest son. You are my very youngest son. I have only two years left in the world. I'm sorry I can't give you education proper. I can't guide you properly. But I bless you. I bless you. I bless you.' That's why every day, I pay my regards to them."

I'm more likely to believe in Superman than the blessings of my parents. I summoned the courage to follow up, but Siddhartha cut me off.

"You have a lot of questions," he said.

"It's because he doesn't know," Meera offered.

I remembered that Shyamal referred to Siddhartha as his "best friend." Truthfully, I had never in my entire life heard my father refer to anyone as a friend. I asked my uncle what his relationship was like with my father when they were children.

"Your father was a very good student. With him, there was always a rivalry relationship between us," Siddhartha said. Meera cackled upon hearing this.

"He was the most favorite for the family among your mother and father," Meera said, referring to my father.

"He was a rival to me. He said, 'Yes.' I always said, 'No.' I said, 'Yes,' always, he said, 'No.' *Every time,* we were in conflict." Siddhartha mused. "He was the mooooost beloved guy of my parents."

Siddhartha grinned as he recounted trying to correct Shyamal in debates when he was younger, only to be rebuked by their parents, who could not believe Shyamal was wrong about something. Ah, so the root cause of that superiority complex my father referred to wasn't difficult to figure out, as I pictured my grandparents saying, *"Our Shyamal? He wouldn't be wrong about anything! Go to your room, Siddhartha!"*

"That relationship converted to love because we are now ancient," Siddhartha said, laughing. "We have love and affection between us. We are friends, rather than brothers. Next question."

"What was his personality?" I said.

"Excellent. Very good," Siddhartha said. He turned his chin slowly to dramatically glimpse at my sleeping father, which got a laugh from us. My uncle wasn't a particularly jovial person. But every now and then he would pull out an unexpected quip, and it made us feel briefly at ease.

Siddhartha opened his mouth and closed it. His eyes moved about the room as he deliberated whether to let loose what was on his mind. Then he looked down sheepishly.

"I can't say anything," he decided.

"Na, na, bolo!" I egged him on in Bengali. ("No, no. Say it!")

"No, no, no, no. But one thing," Siddhartha said.

He stopped for a few seconds and looked directly at us. All I could hear was an oscillating fan going back and forth.

"A man is known as a man by his personality. If you have no personality, you are very much an animal. You understand? Now, go ahead, please," Siddhartha said.

I, what? It seemed best to nod and move on. I asked him about his relationship with Sachindra, my grandfather.

"Wow. Brilliant!" Siddhartha said, before clapping. This was the first time in years of conducting interviews that a subject had applauded a question of mine. I was killing it journalistically, even while feeling slightly fearful of Siddhartha.

"My father was always loving and affectionate toward me because I was the youngest," Siddhartha said. He described how Sachindra would go to court and routinely bring home treats for him. Siddhartha also said that he parented his own two children—my cousins, whom I had never met—in the exact same way.

"That's why my son and daughter highly love me. Every day, they will make FaceTime with us. Your child always follows you. Remember it. Your child always follows you. Because a child always follows his parents," Siddhartha said.

Because a child always follows his parents. I am a prime example of the opposite.

He encouraged me to ask more questions. This felt like a news conference. I racked my brain for what he hadn't told me yet. Siddhartha had, until now, forcefully avoided discussing the less than savory aspects of the Deb family lineage. He was most excited about his loving parents, a perfectly normal sibling rivalry with a brother, and his pride in overcoming adversity. Speaking in a soft, measured voice, I settled on something uncomfortable.

"When my father decided to move back to Kolkata, what was your reaction?" I asked. I thought he might avoid the question, especially with Shyamal in the same room. It might have felt like opening up old wounds and sullying the picture he had painted of our family.

Siddhartha lowered his voice. I could hear the slightest quiver. "I told him not to leave U.S.A. Your two kids are there. Don't come here." He began to crescendo, regaining his authoritative stature. "You can't stay here a long time, because of love and affection. Don't come here. Don't come here. But there are so many reasons he may say to come to India. But I repeatedly told him not to come. You will be sorry because you love your sons highly. You can't live in their absence. But ultimately, he overcame these things."

It was a remarkable and circular thing to say: that my father overcame missing his children whom he chose to leave.

Meera said Shyamal's first four years were a struggle in Kolkata. He didn't have a home and often stayed with Sudhirendra. He had trouble getting accustomed to the hot weather. He considered going to Bangaluru.

"Over time, he felt that he had to stay," Meera said in Bengali.

"It takes a lot of time to adjust. Now he's more Indian than me," Siddhartha said. "But one thing, he is a guy staying alone with purest scale of character. He is a pure man. *He is a pure man!* These are the characteristics of our family."

Shyamal still said nothing. He had his head buried in one hand, half asleep. I was out of questions for the moment, but more than that, I was fatigued. I had learned more about my family in twenty-four hours than I had in thirty years.

After some more small talk, we said our goodbyes to Siddhartha and Meera. I promised we'd keep in touch. They promised they would as well.

Wesley and I touched their feet and we left. Shyamal, for the first time in hours, seemed energized after napping through our visit. And he had some points of his own for us to follow.

TEN

"That country was calling me."

He arrived in windy Rochester, New York, the night of December 1, 1975. It was about nine thirty. The cabdriver who picked him up at the airport was also an engineer but moonlighted as a cabbie to help make ends meet. Shyamal, wearing only a thin overcoat, had never seen snow before. He said he had eight dollars in his pocket. (On this, I'll quote Hasan Minhaj, one of the most prominent comedians of Indian descent in the United States, who said on his Netflix show, *Patriot Act*: "Every immigrant uncle has some insane story about how they came to America with an inexplicably small amount of money." And my father had one too.) America was in a turbulent place: Richard Nixon had resigned the previous year, the Vietnam War had recently ended, and high inflation persisted. Also *Jaws* had created a nationwide fear of mechanical sharks.

My father had a place to stay: an Indian acquaintance who had also come to the United States and happened to live in Rochester.

Shyamal rested for the next twenty-four hours, then started looking for work immediately thereafter. About a month later, having not an ounce of luck nor money, he moved to Queens, where another friend took him in. In early 1976, he got his first job in America as a design engineer for Lorch (now called Smiths Interconnect), an electronics company in Englewood, New Jersey. Shyamal moved to nearby Paterson and lived in the first residence of his own.

Here he settled down and began his pursuit of the American Dream(™), hoping to follow the path of so many other immigrants. A year later, he went to work for the now-defunct Engelmann Microwave Company. He had worked with microwaves back in Kolkata and had some familiarity with the product. (In retrospect, this makes the pinewood derby tragedy even more confusing.) Professionally, Shyamal was finding some comfort, but there was a hole: He was lonely. While he had always seemed to live a life of solitude, at least in India he was surrounded by people who looked like him and shared his culture.

"In America that's not the case," my father said as we sat again at his kitchen table. We had spent some time decompressing from the morning's visit with Siddhartha, and now Shyamal was loudly sipping his coffee.

My father was never *supposed* to be in America; the fact he had even made it there was an accomplishment. His family had other plans for him. And given Shyamal's upbringing, plans weren't suggestions.

The first phase of the plan was school, and the instructions were made clear by his father and then, after his father died, by his brother:

Attend school. Finish at the top of the class. Go to school for engineering. Finish a master's degree.

From a young age, Shyamal didn't have many friends. It wasn't important to him. He was a loner, and an arrogant one at that, by his own admission. He did dress well and took part in group events: Shyamal was good at sports and often performed music in public. But, by his telling, his superiority complex kept him isolated.

"I somehow made myself very choosy," Shyamal said. "I hardly had a friend."

I could relate to my father on this. When I was in elementary and middle school, I didn't have very many friends either. When I sat alone in the corner of the playground during recess, I'd think that I was alone because I was smarter than all of the other kids, not because they didn't want to play with me. It was the friendship equivalent of "You can't fire me. I quit." But the truth is that I was hurt to be playing by myself.

I was relieved whenever I was invited to join the other kids' games. We'd play Superheroes, a game in which we'd all pick a superhero and pretend to fight crime. The other boys would pick folks like Batman and Spider-Man. I'd always pick Captain Picard from *Star Trek: The Next Generation.* I couldn't really help the other guys take on bad guys. I would just give them orders, like a good captain. (Look, I was a strange kid. What do you want me to tell you?)

Whatever Shyamal's feelings were, whether an actual superiority complex, or hurt from not being able to connect with other folks, they lingered to this day.

"Even now, it's like that," my father said.

He gave an example from his tennis game that morning: "Today, for example, a guy I was playing with, a very good player, but he made some comment, and I said, 'If you repeat it, I'm going to get out of this court.' Certain things I don't like. But everybody cannot be like me. This is a bad quality sometimes. I don't know what it is. It has always been my problem. I've been selective of my friends and associates." My father isn't a person who takes slights well.

In the late 1950s, Shyamal arrived in Kolkata, where he attended Jadavpur University, a public school, and graduated with a bachelor's and master's degree in electronics and telecommunications. He called his college experience "super," which is not a word a human being typically uses in a sentence unless he's Clark Kent. Up through his first two years of college, he lived in Sudhirendra's flat—or, as he put it, "under his influence, under his law," as if his oldest brother was a drug or a dictator. Shyamal finished his coursework in 1967 and his thesis in 1968. When I was in high school, he gave me a copy of his thesis, which I still have. He showed great pride in handing it to me, as if proving his worth.

"So what happens after 1968?" I asked.

He stopped and deliberated for a few moments before speaking again.

"That's a good question. That was something I like to keep private, but it was the most dramatic experience of my life, which I do not forget even today," Shyamal said. He turned his head upward but emotionally inward. His voice shook.

Siddhartha had hinted at something like this in our conversation earlier that day.

"What? Dad, I can't write this without you opening up," I said.

Shyamal relented. After graduating from Jadavpur, he received a scholarship to go study in Canada at the University of Calgary, in Alberta, to get his PhD. His other choice was to stay and work a less prestigious job in India. "Unfortunately, I did not get any support from anybody in my family," Shyamal said. "So I took an ordinary job in India." "Ordinary," in this case, by the way, meant working as a run-of-the-mill designer and development engineer in Kolkata. Remember my father's description of himself: a slight superiority complex, a feeling of unique ability. To be one of the crowd did not suit him. He wanted to see a world outside of India. But his family, notably his oldest brother, wanted him to stay. So he did.

"I was demoralized by some people. My youth and inexperience was exploited by my family members," Shyamal said. I could taste the bitterness.

"Why did they want to stop you?" I asked.

"No details on this. It will become a messy story," Shyamal said. "Average person. I didn't want to be average. I knew I was a bright man. But I had other qualities. I was aggressive. I was dynamic. I was forward looking. This did not suit me at all. In that process, I lost the most valuable seven years of my life."

I couldn't get him to divulge more, but I did connect some dots in my own mind between his need to be above average and his conspicuous lack of friendships. He eventually applied to immigrate to the United States in 1975 against the wishes of his family, in the hopes of proving his true worth.

"My mind was set there. Most progressive country. I could use my energy, my strength, my knowledge. I could gain knowledge. That country was calling me every second of my life," Shyamal said.

"Why did the United States call you and not your other brothers and sisters?" I asked.

"At that time, in the 1940s and 1950s, people used to go to England for higher studies. From the 1960s onward, America opened the door for people like us," Shyamal said. (The United States passed legislation in the mid-1960s radically overhauling its immigration system. Instead of basing it on ethnicity-based quotas, the country began favoring attracting skilled workers. This created the contemporary immigration system we know today and the one that would draw my father to leave home.) "The most developed country in the world. Everybody had a dream. Even today, every Indian man has a dream to go to the United States."

Shyamal's family didn't agree with his view at the time. Emigration was an expensive process, and they wouldn't give him the financial support he needed, so he scraped together the money to go himself, with a little help from Siddhartha, his youngest brother. This dynamic reminded me a bit of the scene in *The Godfather: Part II,* when Michael Corleone tells his entire family he's decided to enlist in the war. Everyone reacts with outrage, telling him that he is supposed to do what his father, Vito, has laid out for him. The only person in the room who congratulates Michael and supports him is Fredo.

As I listened to Shyamal talk about his move to the United States, the word "choice" kept popping up in my mind, as if the word was a long-lost friend I had just come to appreciate. It made me think of how differently we approached the concept.

"Choice," as I thought about it in this context, referred to the pursuit of, well, whatever we want. It can be found in the inconsequential. For example, in middle school and high school, I used to watch *Whose Line Is It Anyway?,* the improv show hosted by Drew Carey. There were times when my stomach would hurt from laughing too hard. I considered segments like "Scenes from a Hat," during which the show's cast would perform short scenes in quick bursts suggested by the audience, to be a national treasure. I'd think to myself: *I want to do that someday*. It made sense for a kid who coped with every tense situation by making jokes.

The aspirations were fleeting. Something else was in the cards for me, or so I thought. Maybe I'd be a history teacher. Perhaps I'd pursue the piano and become a musician. Or journalism, because I wanted to be a sports broadcaster. Becoming the brown Mike Breen seemed like an ideal life for me.

I pondered what life I would choose for myself. *For myself.* It being my choice was such a given that outside interference didn't even enter my mind. If I wanted to become an improv comedian, I could've joined a troupe on campus and then, in theory, devoted my life to finding stage time. If being a musician was how I wanted to spend my life, I could have auditioned for music programs around the country or outside the United States and let the chips fall where they may. If I followed through on sports broadcasting, after graduating college, I could have started calling minor league baseball games and worked my way up.

Instead, I chose to go a different route, which is how I ended up at the *Boston Globe* after college. Eventually, I chose to leave television altogether. And who knows what happens next? Maybe, by some twist of fate, I do end up as Mike Breen, just hopefully not broadcasting Knicks games like he does. I'm a masochist, but even I have standards.

The career choices I took for granted all through my life were opportunities my father never had. In some ways, yes, I had a difficult upbringing. But I was able to take much of my future into my own hands, in part because of the autonomy I had because of the rockiness at home. Dealing with the fallout from my parents' lack of choice gave me the strength to carve my own path, whether choosing a college or a profession. I never even asked my parents before making critical life decisions. I just made them.

Many of my friends brought up in America have similar stories. They might have consulted with their parents about future plans, but it was always ultimately up to them. And this is not to say that all parents in India still demand of their children what my grandparents did. Look at Manvi, whose wedding we would attend in a few days. But choice is a ubiquitous concept for Western children. I don't mean that in a preachy-rah-rah-let's-celebrate-America-and-freedom-on-July-4th-with-Lee-Greenwood kind of way. Freedom is great, of course, but it's different than what I'm referring to. This is about choice: the agency to have the space, independent of familial pressures, to pursue your own fulfillment. It's unlike anything with which my parents were familiar. After hearing Shyamal's story, I cherished it a bit more.

Shyamal did try to take some control of his own destiny, but it took a superhuman effort of his own in defying his family to come to the United States and build himself up from scratch to survive. In many ways, I had started from ahead. For one thing, I was born and brought up in middle-class America. My life has been a struggle to connect, not a struggle to sustain myself. Shyamal and, as I would later find out, Bishakha had to deal with both.

"I became desperate," Shyamal said. "People tried to discourage me again and stop my going. I said, 'No.'" I respected him for this. It's what I would have done.

"The steering wheel was in my hand," Shyamal said.

In New Jersey, Shyamal set out to look for a life partner to make the loneliness less overwhelming. He put an ad in a newspaper called *Bharat Matrimony* (*Bharat* means India), which is now a website that allows you to complete a Soulmate Search™. Shyamal's ad, which he published in 1977, was in the American version of the paper produced out of New York.

One of the sample ads on the present-day website reads:

Telugu Male 28 M.Tech. (IIT) going to US soon Executive in PSU seeks Professional girl Christian / Hindu any Contact: 040-xxx xxxx (Kannan) xxx-xxx xxx4. Email:xxxxxxxx@vsnl.com write to Box No. C-xxxx, Indian Express, Lalbaug Industrial Estate, Lalbaug, Mumbai-12.

Shyamal's ad was similar: name, age, profession, salary, PO

Box number. Responses started coming in immediately. A dozen prospective wives, many of them students, responded.

"Most of them, I did not like," Shyamal said. In twenty-first-century parlance, he swiped left. "One person, I met. She was older than me. I didn't go for it."

He put up a second advertisement. Again, several women responded. One was a fellow engineer. Shyamal didn't take kindly to her. "I'm selective. I expect some characteristics of everybody. If it's not there, I cannot stay with them. I could not live with them even for a week," Shyamal said.

Okay, so maybe he *was* choosy.

"So what were you looking for in somebody?" I asked.

"You don't know your father at all," Shyamal said. "I wanted to be with somebody who has some flavor in life, who has some education, some family value, and some professionalism. And at least 60 percent my culture in the sense."

"You wanted someone Bengali?" I offered, wondering what the "60 percent" referred to.

He nodded.

"It was many things," he said. "Your life is what you've built yourself. Your parents will give you the seed. But you have to build yourself. In that building process, you build your personality. There you have some likes and dislikes. Certain areas you can compromise, other places you cannot." This was the closest thing I'd ever had to a sex talk with Shyamal.

At some point, Shyamal received a response to his ad from my grandmother in Toronto on my mother's side. There was a letter that was written to my father giving Bishakha's background, with a picture attached. He was impressed by the letter. It matched what he was looking for.

"I was desperate to get a partner at that time," Shyamal said. He might have been picky, but his feelings of isolation had made him increasingly forlorn.

He flew to Toronto, where my mother's family was living. Shyamal said Bishakha was staying there with her younger brother, Atish, and her mother, Amiya. Bishakha was supporting all three of them by herself.

"I just liked her," Shyamal said. "She was everything I wanted in life. And at one point, I said, 'The last ten years, I'm looking for a girl. It's the first time I got a girl like you.'"

But this wasn't the ending of *You've Got Mail*. You couldn't hear the UB40 version of "(I Can't Help) Falling in Love with You" blaring in the distance. There was a catch: To Shyamal's shock, Bishakha did not know that her mother had reached out to my father about a prospective marriage. He showed up at her family's door after having spent the money to fly to Toronto, not a cheap flight. It was my grandmother and my uncle Atish who greeted Shyamal. Bishakha didn't know who he was or why he was there. She had no interest in getting married. Not to Shyamal. Not to anybody else.

"When she saw me in their house, she realized something was going on," Shyamal said. "She said nothing."

My mother's silence surprised him. He didn't know my mother didn't want to marry him.

"When I left, I told her, 'I'll call you tomorrow, and we should meet again,'" Shyamal said, recalling the end of their first visit.

My father did, indeed, contact her the next day. The phone call went to Bishakha's job; she worked as a switchboard operator.

"She was reluctant to speak to me," Shyamal said.

At the urging of Atish and my grandmother, Bishakha met Shyamal for dinner at a restaurant. My father didn't remember the exact type of food, other than that it was "Western." Dinner was enjoyable enough, and the next day, Shyamal invited Bishakha to go to Niagara Falls with another couple he was friends with who lived in Toronto. She acquiesced.

I asked him to describe that trip, and, in response, my father pointed to Wesley and me. "Just like you are enjoying her company. Same almost. Same magnitude," he said of his trip to Niagara Falls.

"Hopefully not quite like that," I quipped.

The jaunt went reasonably well, even though my mother still didn't want to get married. The stakes were high: Niagara Falls was Shyamal's chance to win my mother over. It was their first instance of spending extended time together. For Shyamal in particular, he wasn't going to be lonely for a weekend and perhaps for a lifetime. The trip was probably the first and last time my parents were happy together.

Before I quizzed more, Shyamal began to grow weary of the questioning.

"Do I have to tell you about all these things?" Shyamal said.

"Yes," I said.

"Why?" Shyamal said. His voice became harder.

"Because it's important to me," I said.

"Why?" he repeated.

"Why is it important to me? Because it's important to me," I answered parsimoniously. It was the only way I knew how to handle tense conversations, aside from cracking jokes.

"You're writing a book," Shyamal said.

"The book is important to me and listening to this conversation is important to me," I said. My frustration was growing.

"Do I have to meet all your demands, even though you're my dearest son?" Shyamal said.

"Yes, for this particular case, yes. It's important to me," I said.

"Why is it important to you?" Shyamal asked for a third time.

"Because it's important to me," I growled. "I came all the way here."

"You did not come to write a book. You came to see me," Shyamal said. You could almost see that on the tip of his tongue, he wanted to add, "Right?" But he didn't say it. Maybe he thought I'd say no. But I was determined. I wanted to be able to have a regular conversation with my father *so badly*. I didn't want the artificial barriers anymore. I wanted explanations. I wanted something real.

"Do you understand that normal families are able to talk about these things?" I exploded. Wesley was silent this whole time.

"I've never said this to anybody," Shyamal said. We were both stubborn.

"Do you understand that these are the kinds of things I need to know about?" I said.

"No, you do not," Shyamal said. "Nobody in the world understood what was going through my mind."

"I'm trying to understand it!" I said. "You telling me basics isn't informative or helpful to me at all."

I was being unreasonable; he didn't actually owe me every part of himself. He was trying to be informative, to shed light on episodes I had never heard of. It should have been enough.

"On the whole, we liked each other. We got married. That's it," Shyamal said. I think, in his own way, he was trying not to say hurtful things about Bishakha.

"Stop saying that!" I said, nearly shouting. "That's not it. My childhood was miserable. Do you understand that?"

"I do," Shyamal said, without a second's hesitation.

"Do you understand how unhappy my brother and I were growing up in that household?" I said. I could feel my blood boiling. Thirty years of anger were pouring out of me, and I couldn't do anything but watch it.

"Yes," Shyamal said.

"Do you know how little I know about you and Mom?" I said.

"Yes, I know that," Shyamal said.

"I need to understand how this happened," I said. "I need to know everything."

"As a father, did I ever neglect you?" Shyamal asked. "Were you deprived of any love from your father within his human capacity? From my side, did I leave any stone unturned from any aspect as a father?"

"I would say yes," I answered. Did I mean it? I was letting years of exasperation seep out. "I have gone my whole life without answers to basic questions." I pounded the table. "Now it's your turn. Now you have to answer them. I don't care about anything else. I don't care that I own this flat. You need to answer questions. Questions that you're not going to be around too much longer to answer."

These were hurtful things for me to say, but Shyamal sat there, occasionally clenching his fists but otherwise expressionless. There was a tinge of sadness in his face. He didn't try to interrupt or look away. He was a willing punching bag for my verbal swings, encouraging me without saying a word. He wasn't angry, just tired and resigned. The coffee cup in front of him was empty. But I wasn't done.

"And I'm telling you right now, I'm not gonna be like that with my kids, okay?" I said. "I will not. I'm not gonna hold things back from them, the way that you and Mom have with my brother and me, okay? I don't want the relationship with us to be the relationship that you had with your father, okay? We need to be able to talk about this stuff, it's important. You need to be open right now."

And to Shyamal's credit, he had been somewhat open before I berated him. But now, something had changed between us. We both knew it. I had never seen my father look this vulnerable or stung in my life. And we hadn't even covered the most difficult topic yet.

Many of his choices still left me perplexed. Right from their wedding day in 1977, a few months after they met, there was simmering hostility. Their ceremony was a small one in New York, in front of about fifty guests. Shyamal began changing jobs which meant changing states. First there was a move to Florida. While they were there, Sattik was born, in 1979. Then came moves to Virginia and Massachusetts.

I came in 1988. In the early 1990s, the Deb family moved back to New Jersey, when I was about three. Shyamal, who already thought of himself as discerning, thought Bishakha was cold and lacked ambition. Neither felt they could have the intelligent conversations the other desired out of a life partner. Bishakha, who hadn't wanted to get married in the first place, sank into a depression that slowly got worse as the marriage went on. They each viewed the other as domineering, demanding, and unable to empathize.

This dynamic always existed. So there was an obvious and rather existential question I had to pose: "Why did you decide to have a second child if things were already bad?"

"I was very happy when you were born," Shyamal said.

"I believe you, but—" I began to answer, but he interrupted.

"No. I was very happy when you were born. Any father in the world will love their children," Shyamal said. "When you were born, there was a difference of nine years between the two of you: 1979 and 1988. I loved both of you in the deepest core of my heart. Life is not about mathematics. It can happen to anybody. When you came, I was very happy to see you."

"I'm not saying you didn't love me as a kid. When I was conceived, was I planned?" I said. Now we were literally having a sex talk.

"Hard to say," Shyamal said. He looked up at the ceiling

and thought some more. He repeated it again. Shyamal said they were always planning on having a second child, but it was unclear whether my mother's health would allow it. But I also wasn't sure my father understood the question. For my parents, having children wasn't even a decision. It was just something they were supposed to do. It's what their family members would've done. I was born of two parents who had limited control over their futures growing up but who *chose* to have me, in spite of the contempt they had for one another. And my father couldn't even explain why.

Given how unhealthy they were together, was it responsible for them to have a second child? Don't get me wrong, I'm glad I exist. But should I?

ELEVEN

"My dearest son, I have no regret."

When I was in elementary school, I became obsessed with professional wrestling. I had to watch in secret though, because I knew my parents wouldn't approve of me idolizing oiled-up grown men who fake-hit each other with metal chairs. My favorite performer was this guy Paul Wight, better known today as Big Show. Wight is less a guy and more the human manifestation of an oil tanker, at one point in his career clocking in at more than four hundred pounds. Every time he entered the ring, his opponents would quake with fear (or, you know, pretend to). A single punch from him would cartoonishly launch opponents to the other side of the ring. And if they weren't being slammed to the canvas, Big Show would headbutt them to another dimension.

At home, I used to take multiple pillows, stuff them inside each other, and create dummies to bodyslam. I created elaborate scenarios where I would "fight" A-list wrestlers like Kane, the

Undertaker, and my favorite, Big Show. My finishing move was "the Hellraiser," which involved putting a pillow in a headlock, lifting it up over my right shoulder, and then piledriving it into the mat, which was, in this case, my bed.

I didn't have wrestling tights, so I used to run around in only my underwear. It was a bizarre sight for both of my parents, who knew little about half-naked men fake-fighting each other as a form of entertainment, or that I even watched them. I composed my own theme song on the keyboard, which was not bad, actually, and I delivered promos with an imaginary microphone.

"HEY BIG SHOW! WHEN SOPAN DEB GETS YOU IN THE RING, HE'S GOING TO RAIIIISEEEE SOMEEEE HELLLL!"

I gravitated to performers like Big Show because he was everything I wasn't. I was scrawny and afraid of actual physical confrontations. Hey, you would be too if you were my size. Put me against someone with a heartbeat? I'm the guy seeing my life flash in front of my eyes as Big Show enters the ring. No more raising hell for me.

I have, however, been in one physical altercation in my life that didn't involve my parents. It was during eighth grade, that year where my mother had locked herself in her room and it was just Shyamal taking care of me. There was this one classmate I had—we'll call him Gary—who was not well liked by anybody. He was always making inappropriate and demeaning comments to those around him. Gary was troubled and not well adjusted at an already difficult age for boys. He was disruptive in class, and his frequent antics seemed to come from a place of malice. I'm almost two decades older now, and in hindsight, it's clear Gary was battling some demons that even he didn't understand at the time. Come to think of it, I was too.

One morning, we were milling around in the classroom

waiting for the first class of the day to start. I was in the back of the room doing something, maybe playing on the computer, when Gary made some unprovoked comment toward me. It was something derogatory about a turban. I didn't hear him at first, but he repeated it. This was shortly after the September 11, 2001, terrorist attacks. Every now and then, some other students would say it was my relatives who flew a plane into the World Trade Center.

I cannot say this enough: I was scrawny. I never picked fights. But something came over me in this moment. The backdrop of my home life had put me in such an angry place. And manliness was very much a topic of discussion among the cool kids. I'd hear classmates talk with great admiration about fights that others got into and the toughness with which they fought. I was uncool but desired very much to be the opposite. In this moment, I thought that getting into a fight would raise my status.

I walked to the front of the classroom, where Gary was standing, and I clocked him in the face. A right hook to his left cheek. My classmates were stunned. Gary, after initially falling backward over a chair, was also stunned. I stared at my fists as if a comic book movie villain had taken control of them.

Gary ran out of the classroom to tell a teacher, and I was immediately taken to a vice principal's office, where I offered my side of the story. Our reputations were weighed: I had never been in a fight in school, but Gary had. While I was known for acting up in class, I had great grades. Gary didn't. It was believable that Gary was the instigator.

When the decision was made to suspend me for two days and him for at least a couple more, maybe a week, the vice principal called Shyamal to tell him what happened and that he had to come pick me up from school. My father would have to leave work early.

Remember how I never called my parents to tell them I had been arrested while covering Trump? Let me tell you: You definitely don't want to be the brown kid who calls his parents to tell them about a school suspension. Ever.

In Shyamal's car we were silent the entire ride. He didn't ask what happened, and I didn't try to explain. I was steeling myself to be told what a disappointment I was. How I would never get into college. How a school suspension is the equivalent of a felony. But there were no words, not even from the radio.

Shyamal was expressionless. Instead of turning toward our house, he drove toward Route 9, the local highway, and he kept driving. I thought this was the end of my life. He was going to murder me. After about twenty-five minutes of driving, he turned right onto an exit ramp. We entered a parking lot I knew well in Freehold, a neighboring town. This shopping plaza had the Freehold Grand Buffet, a bloated Chinese restaurant and one of my favorite dining establishments. Shyamal exited the car and walked toward the restaurant. He was still quiet. I followed him.

Maybe this is the last meal before the execution, I thought.

The restaurant was mostly empty, since most folks were at school or at work. After the waiter took our drink orders, we went to the buffet to get food. I loaded up my plate. If this was to be my last meal, I was headed to the afterlife on a full stomach.

When we sat back down, Shyamal looked intently at me. Speaking softly, he said that he understood why I reacted the way I did to what Gary said. But he also said that I was wrong, that I should never have laid hands on him. *No matter what Gary said.* At the end of the day, a racist crack from a thirteen-year-old wasn't more dangerous than a sucker punch to the face.

He said all of this without a hint of malice in his voice. He wasn't trying to guilt me. Instead, he took on the soft demeanor of a professor. Shyamal was trying to use this as a teaching moment, yet all I felt was confusion. *He should be angry at me. Why is he downplaying this?* In a very Admiral Ackbar voice, I said to myself, *It's a traaaaaaaap.*

Several minutes passed, and my mind-set realigned. I went from puzzlement to shame. Instead of being angry, Shyamal was empathetic, a side I rarely saw. I realized he was right, and the school administration was wrong. Gary shouldn't have been suspended after getting punched in the face and then telling a teacher about it. I was wrong. There was no excuse for my behavior.

Shyamal put that in perspective for me right away. He was calm, which did not give me the opportunity to get defensive. He was soothing, but stern. It was his greatest moment as a father, although, like many things he did, it went unappreciated at the time.

Weeks later, I walked upstairs from my basement and I watched my father getting into a police car. It was the last time we lived together.

Seventeen years had passed since that buffet conversation, and there was a piece of the puzzle still nagging at me. Sitting at my father's kitchen table in another hemisphere, this was my chance to clear it up.

I needed to find out why he'd left the country—but it was he who began.

"Let me ask a simple question," Shyamal said. "Last ten years, I've been in India. How many phone calls have I made to you during this period? It's a very important point. I've made more than two hundred phone calls to you. Did any one of you bother to give me a call to find out whether I'm dead or alive? No."

Shyamal said that one year prior to our visit, he had come down with dengue fever, an epidemic that was spreading through Kolkata at the time.

"I was in the hospital," Shyamal said. "I could've been dead. If not for my brother, I would've been dead."

"I think you don't understand that when you left for India you did not give any information as to why you left," I said. "You just left. We kept calling."

Shyamal kept trying to protest, but I wouldn't let him.

"You're going to let me finish," I said, uncharacteristically firm.

I recounted the exchange of emails, from when I woke up one morning weeks after his visit to my college campus to an email saying that he was sick and had to leave the country. "And then I asked when you were coming back. You said you didn't know, and then you never came back. And you expect me to just drop everything for a father that I barely know, that I grew up in an unhappy household with, that barely knows anything about me?" I said. "I'm watching my friends grow up. They're having their dads coach them in baseball. My dad wasn't doing any of that stuff."

"Correct," Shyamal answered.

"You expect, after everything that I saw growing up, for me to just drop everything I was doing, when I had to really fend for myself for a lot of my childhood?" I said.

"The only reason me and your mother stayed together—only one reason," Shyamal said.

"To have children?" I said.

"My children must have love, care, and affection and then grow up," he said, wistfully. "Within my human capacity, I've done everything I could."

When Shyamal moved out of our house in Howell, he got

an apartment about thirty minutes away. I remember visiting it once: It was almost entirely empty. There was one dingy couch placed across from a small television in a living room with a hardwood floor. There was a desk. I remember thinking it was the embodiment of sadness. Those walls told a tragic story about my father. I didn't want to visit again.

In describing his life there, Shyamal repeated his line from when he described his dengue fever: Nobody checked to see if he was dead or alive. I certainly rarely did. But despite this, Shyamal vowed to keep supporting my brother and me, at least from his telling.

"I'm the head of the family. I did my part. I didn't expect anything in return. That was my attitude," Shyamal said.

He continued: "After coming to India, doctors said I couldn't do anything about it."

"Do anything about what?" I said.

"That's the problem. You never knew what was going on in my life," Shyamal said.

"I don't understand why you had to come to India," I said.

I felt like I was opening the vault of our family trauma. For years, I thought I'd never get an answer. And here I was on the precipice. Shyamal hesitated. Again. He said it was a story he had never told anybody.

The last time I saw my father before he left, his health had been deteriorating from various forms of stress. At one point, unknown to me, he was hospitalized for almost a week with a fever that wouldn't come down. There was severe financial strain from being laid off the year before from AT&T, and the prospects of future employment, given his age, were grim. What also contributed to his physical and mental health struggles was the fact he was living alone, with no one to look after him and no other family around. Both his sons, already distant from their father, were focused on their own lives.

Amid this, and just after our visit, Shyamal got into a car accident. When he was driving, he said, sometimes he'd black out. In this instance, there was a crash, but airbags saved his life. He called Somnath, his nephew, to come pick him up at the hospital. But this was a disastrous move, as it turned out. When he got home that night, he passed out in his bathroom and woke up there several hours later.

"I stood up and said, 'From home, I'm going to live. And from home, I'm going to die,'" Shyamal said. "I had to make a choice: either a graveyard in America or come back and take the help of your family and survive."

So he left, a broken man unable to see a life for himself in America anymore. He needed to be home with the family he had in Kolkata for his own mental health. He thought I would never look out for him. Once again, Shyamal would leave family behind against their wishes to go abroad.

"Listen carefully: When you board an aircraft, the steward gives the lecture. She explains if something happens in the aircraft, what do you do? You put the oxygen mask on your mouth. And then what does she say? Before you help the child, you must put the oxygen mask on your mouth first. Because if you're dead, you cannot help anyway," Shyamal said.

My father leaned forward ever so slightly and squeezed his fists. But his tone was stern. It pierced through the hum of the running air-conditioner. He did not equivocate in letting me know how alone he felt at the time.

He was describing his decision as an altruistic act. But I would argue it had to do as much with self-preservation as it did with selflessness. My father, if I were to guess, has a deep desire to take control of his own destiny. Growing up in India with a domineering father and, after he passed, an equally strict eldest living brother didn't make that easy for him. Coming to America, a land of what he saw as limitless opportunity, was his pathway to fulfillment, but so was leaving it. Shyamal felt like he was dying in the United States. The depression he was feeling from a lifetime of disconnects, in combination with the financial stress, weighed on him like an anchor. He needed a restart.

"If I died there," he said, referring to the United States, "none of you would come perform my last rituals. None of you! The best decision of my life was to get out of this."

I never knew about the car accident. But Shyamal asked the same piercing question again. "Did anybody care to know? Including yourself?"

"When I didn't hear from you for a couple of weeks, I was very worried," I said quietly, inwardly ashamed. It was like we were at the Chinese restaurant all over again after I punched my classmate. How could I, as a son, ever let our relationship get to that point? As an adult? *As a human?* My own father didn't think anyone loved him enough to care if he died or not. The bare minimum that a father (and a mother) should expect from a son is to feel cared for; to live the back half of your life knowing that you aren't alone. As I thought about this, I didn't look away from Shyamal's face. For the first time, I noticed his wrinkles. They seemed to etch out a map. When I first arrived in India, my father's unexpected youthfulness stuck out. In this moment, I was reminded that he was older, that he was mortal. But even still, I remained defensive. This wasn't just my fault. It couldn't be. Could it?

"I think it's totally reasonable for a nineteen-year-old to be surprised that his dad just moved to another country out of nowhere," I said. That's when, for the first time in my life, I decided to take some responsibility for my part in our family's disconnect. "I will say that when I was in high school, I should have called more."

"Should have what?" Shyamal said.

"I should have called more," I admitted.

"Called?" Shyamal said. He seemed like he didn't understand what I was saying, like he couldn't comprehend this contrition on my part.

"I should have called more. You. I should have called you more," I repeated.

He seemed taken aback. "Every day, after the end of our dinners, I used to hug you. I am your father. Every day, I wanted to do my duty more because now he's a helpless man. I used to go and attend your high school performances. I loved it. I was so proud of you," Shyamal recalled, adding, "I cannot hug you every day. I miss it very much. But I was concerned about your future very much. I didn't know what to do."

I brought up the story of going to the Chinese restaurant with him after I punched Gary. I said it was my fondest memory with him (though the pinewood derby comes close). The Chinese restaurant wasn't a *happy* memory. It wasn't pretty. But it was my father being a parent.

"Yes, yes. Very good, you remember it, yes?" Shyamal said. He softened his voice and looked away. For a split second, I thought he might have disappeared into his own recollection of that lunch.

"Of course I do. But I wish we had more moments like that. We didn't have many of those," I said. "I should have reached out to you more growing up."

"But you were a small kid," Shyamal interrupted.

"Let me finish. When you guys got divorced when I was in high school, you have to understand that all I associated with you and mom was negativity," I said.

"Naturally," he said.

"Just anger and sadness. I just wanted to separate myself from it. That was probably irresponsible of me, but I was young."

"No, no, no. You were very young. Everybody is confused. I am confused!" Shyamal said. Watching my father try to lift the blame off me was touching, but I wasn't going to let him do it.

"When I got to college, I had to handle a lot by myself. After college, I agree. I should have checked in more," I said.

It wasn't enough, but perhaps it never would be. I should've apologized for being so petulant during the time he took care of me in eighth grade. Or for all the missed calls. Or for not knowing he was in a car accident.

"My dearest son, I have no regret," Shyamal said.

That much was clear. After more than a decade in India, he had peace of mind. He was at home in Kolkata.

"There were a lot of times that I wish you were still there," I said. "I wish you had been there when I graduated college. I wish you had been there to see me do stand-up comedy. I wish you could be there to take a tour of the *New York Times*."

He nodded, though his face remained expressionless. If I was to guess, he had those same thoughts himself when he was alone. But he also deserved better from me too. No one should ever feel they don't matter.

Shyamal had never mattered to me as much as he did right in that second. His gaze once again drifted away. I could tell his mind was traveling, but to where I wasn't sure. Maybe through time. Maybe he was picturing me as a child. Or maybe he was picturing the last time we saw each other before I came to India, when I was a rail-thin freshman eating Thai food at a campus restaurant.

"I feel guilty. Guilt feeling was there," my father said. Clearly, he had some regrets, contrary to him saying he had none.

"Particularly somebody is growing up without a father, which I hated. I hated it from the core of my heart. I wanted to do more for my children but I couldn't do it."

I was done. I had asked all the questions I needed to get through, and we both needed a reprieve. He walked into the kitchen and cracked open a Kingfisher, pouring glasses for the three of us. Half a world away from where the fissures between he and I had formed, they began to heal. I sat on my father's couch, sipping his beer, forgiving him for everything. I didn't realize I was doing so, but in the minutes before falling asleep that night, I felt a new sense of tranquillity. I had begun to let go of my anger toward him. It was time.

TWELVE

"The lights of my life are not around me."

With our days in Kolkata running short, Shyamal wanted to show us every inch of his home city and giddily share the historical significance of each stone, statue, and building. Ever set in his routine, he mapped out to the minute what our schedule would be. Sleep, rest, sanity, and flexibility be damned.

The rainy season didn't offer ideal sightseeing weather, but it provided a nice respite from the heat. The museums were indoors, but finding a room with air-conditioning was rare. In the Indian Museum, I stood by an enormous painting of British colonizers for an extended period, staring up, just basking in . . . the breeze from a nearby fan. A Jain temple made entirely of carved, sun-drenched marble was breathtaking, as was walking on said marble as it scorched our bare feet. Our stop at the Marble Palace, a two-story colonial mansion dating back to the 1800s with an odd hodgepodge of junk, valuable art, and an aviary, required the car to wade through two feet of standing water to get us inside.

We went back to the Queen Victoria Memorial in the daytime. Much like our previous nighttime visit, we spent more time posing for pictures for Shyamal than looking at artifacts. *Walk! No, keep walking! Good, good, good, good, good.* As tired and balmy as we were, neither of us could burst his bubble. He was pure joy.

But I was most interested in a simple building that wasn't a landmark. This one had two blue doors that swung open as we drove by. There were multiple clotheslines hanging outside, with sheets currently being soaked by the steady drizzle. Grated windows surrounded the front entrance, and there was a lone wooden bench directly outside the doorway. Two men stood in the doorway working with a cloth of some sort. It seemed to be a shop, with a sign hanging above with Bengali lettering on it.

I had requested a slight detour to stop by this place. My father grudgingly obliged. It had been Shyamal's home in Kolkata when he first arrived from Bangladesh. He didn't offer a walk down memory lane, but I was there, watching my father as a young man walk out those blue doors to make something of himself.

We had skipped only one of Shyamal's planned excursions, but I was starting to feel guilty about it. Earlier in the week, Shyamal had suggested that Wesley and I come watch one of his thrice-weekly games of tennis. Tennis was, it seemed to us, his best evidence that he was leading a happy and full life in India. He wanted me to be proud of him, I think.

When we realized his game was at six in the morning, I reflexively told him that it was not doable. His gracious response couldn't hide the twinge of disappointment in his voice. I quickly rescinded my answer and said that Wesley and I would try and make it. Of course, that conversation happened in the middle of the day. When the time came, we overslept and missed his game.

On our penultimate day in Kolkata, Wesley suggested we

make it up to him. We may have missed out on watching his tennis match, but could he and I play together?

When I popped the question, Shyamal's eyes widened. "You want to play tennis with me?" he said.

I answered in the affirmative. This was an item that had been on my list for a lifetime: to bond with my father over a sport. The anxieties of my childhood were mostly in the rearview mirror, but it wasn't too late to find common ground on the clay court. I knew Shyamal was well trained at this point, having had a coach and playing three times a week for the last decade. The last time I played was in elementary school, and even that was brief. This would be a blowout.

"Oh boy, I'll tell you, Sopan. I'm thrilled that I'll play tennis with you," Shyamal said, followed by his crisp chortle. He kept saying, "This is the dream of my life!"

"Yeah, it'll be great," I said warily. "I'm not very good. I haven't played in many years."

"All right. To play with your father, you don't have to be any good," Shyamal said. "I'm not good either." He was being nice.

I've never been much of an athlete. Freshman year of high school, I tried out for the basketball team. I didn't make it—not an easy feat, considering how atrocious the Howell High School basketball team was. (I distinctly remember trying to steal the ball from a teammate during tryouts, which, while a bold strategy, did not bode well for my chances.)

Baseball wasn't my sport either. Though I was dominant in Little League for one year in sixth grade, I found out it was because Bishakha accidentally placed me in the wrong age group. I was going up against third-graders and looked like the Indian Babe Ruth. The next year, the situation was rectified. I quit after a handful of games because I kept striking out.

Maybe I needed something more grounded. For a brief period

in elementary school, my mother made me take up wrestling. This wasn't the kind where I threw around pillows at home. It was actual competition requiring outmuscling other humans. When the other kids were horsing around and grappling before practice, I would jump in and act as the referee of the exchanges so I wouldn't have to take part in the actual grappling. You get the point. There's a trend here.

When I woke up at the crack of dawn the next day to prepare for my tennis match against Shyamal, I didn't have high hopes. I hadn't swung a racket in twenty years. Even though Shyamal was about to kick my ass, this was about showing up for him.

My father had fretted over the possibility that the game would be rained out, but the weather was perfect when we arrived at the courts. He had on a white polo shirt and a matching baseball cap, and he'd rented a racket for me to use for the day. He also hired a ball boy assigned specifically to our game. We took our places on opposite sides of the court and began. Wesley sat on the court right behind Shyamal. In many tennis matches, this might be a dangerous spot. Not in this case.

My forehands, if you could call them that, sent the tennis ball flying well outside the lines. Every couple of minutes, I'd put my hands up to signal "My bad!" which should have been "I am bad!" I was swinging my racket like a baseball bat. The poor ball boy was sweating profusely, as he was unexpectedly receiving the biggest workout among the three of us, having to chase after all my errant swings.

There was one other issue, though: Shyamal was terrible too. Really bad. I mean, so was I, but I had an excuse. This was not a grand display of tennis on either side. This was the opposite of Borg vs. McEnroe. It was more like two Muppets facing off. I stopped feeling bad for the ball boy once I saw him openly laughing at some of our volleys. Shyamal would trot from one side of the court to the other, flailing at my serves, which were surprising each time they made it over the net.

When Shyamal told me a day earlier that he wasn't good, I thought he was trying to be polite. He wasn't! He actually was terrible. What was his coach teaching him the whole time? Now I had some suspicions about my father's claims of being a strong athlete when he was growing up.

If this experience was about searching for answers, I got the most concrete one this morning: Why wasn't I good at sports? It was in the Deb family blood. Or, rather, talent *wasn't*. After an hour, our clothes were damp with sweat. We mercifully ended our eyesore of a match. Neither of us kept score, but we didn't need to. We both lost.

"If you're out of practice, your focus is not right," Shyamal said as we walked back to my hotel, to which I laughed. He was still beaming with pride. "In a few minutes, I found you getting your grip of it. Initially, the ball was going South Pole and North Pole. As you started playing, you're getting the grip back. If you practice for one month, you'll get the full grip back." (He loved the pole analogy.)

Later that day, we returned to Shyamal's flat one more time before leaving Kolkata. I didn't know how he felt, but, for me, the time we spent together there had brought him to life in my story. I was consumed by the question of when—*or if*—I would see him again after this trip. I knew we would reunite in Delhi in a few days, but leaving his home had a sense of finality for me. He was more than my DNA now. He was my father. But what would Shyamal mean to my kids, if and when I have them? I didn't want them to be surprised by a picture of their grandparents in our home in the way I was at his brother Siddhartha's house. I want my children to have something from their grandparents that is theirs. The same goes for Sattik's two children, who have never met him. I thought it best to let Shyamal decide what he wanted to pass on.

Shyamal walked into the living room and sat on the couch, asking how we were enjoying the scotch he had given us. Nearby, Wesley turned the camera on her phone toward my father.

"I want you to tape a message to your grandchildren. What advice do you have?" I asked Shyamal.

"Ah, yes, unfortunately I won't see them. A few things here. You and Sattik are original Indian blood. Both parents are Indians. The next generation are mixed. It's very natural," he said. "They will look different. They will think different. But the combination of two genes will make them smarter. Yes! Science believes that."

I laughed. I wasn't looking for advice on genetic engineering.

"They may or may not experience some problems as they grow up with their peers. It's your responsibility as parents to explain to them what is their background," he continued. "For example, they must know the rich culture and heritage of India. One of the oldest cultures of the world. It is your responsibility to teach them."

Perhaps he didn't understand what I wanted him to do. "I meant, what is your advice to the kids?" I pressed.

"They must have that knowledge of both sides," Shyamal said. He was referring to both Indian and American culture. His big worry was that the next generation of the Deb bloodline wouldn't know anything about where they came from because they would likely be brought up in the United States.

"They should learn it positively, not be forced to learn it. They have every reason to be proud of the Indian heritage, which is more than four thousand years old. That is my only advice. They should not forget their Indian heritage," he went on.

His advice, on its face, wasn't about how to live life or how to treat people. It was about academics. It was about culture. I was a bit frustrated that this was all he wanted to say. Our disparate understandings of the question, though, were emblematic of the rift that had always been between us. It wasn't malicious on his part or mine, but neither of us could understand how the other sees family and love.

The conversation moved slowly in a more helpful direction.

"You, for example, were excited to find out where I spent my student days," Shyamal said. "This was not true ten years back."

He was correct. Ten years ago, I would not have cared.

"But something came from inside," Shyamal said.

"What about how they should act? How they should behave?" I asked. I was trying again. I wanted him to say something about kindness, respect, that kind of stuff.

"That's the only thing I can tell them," Shyamal said.

"What do you want them to know about you?" Wesley offered.

"Me? Simple man. Came to United States with eight dollars in his pocket. Self-made man. Determination. Never broke down. Went through a lot of struggle. Temperature minus-ten degrees. The very next day I went to look for a job. That's how I started," Shyamal said. "Why? Life of an immigrant. I had to climb a mountain with many obstacles in front of me. But I never got discouraged. I went forward."

This is when it hit me. Right there, in that second, is when I realized what he wanted to pass on. It was *himself.* When he said that his grandchildren "should not forget their Indian heritage," he wanted us to remember him. My father didn't want to be forgotten as the Deb bloodline continued through the generations, which is what likely would have happened had we not seen each other again. This was his way of telling us that he didn't want my children to think of him as irrelevant, in the way I did with his parents. And he didn't want to outright admit it, perhaps out of shame or embarrassment, so he disguised his explanation.

"Are you happy now?" I asked Shyamal. It was a loaded question, in part because happiness is such a vague concept, and one with which my father wasn't intimately familiar. This query had weighed on me since our kitchen table conversations. Being at peace is different than being happy. He seemed at ease with himself and the decisions he had made. But I wondered if he was happy.

"That's a very good question. Let me answer it carefully," he said. "I've wanted to do a lot of things, especially learning in India. Indian civilization. The Mughals. Ancient Indian history. All these things. It was always in the back of my mind for the last fifty years. I want to learn these things. Time flies very fast. You want to learn Indian culture? You have to live in India."

This was a question about visceral emotions, but Shyamal could only answer in the abstract; an engineer explaining his method.

"When I came to India, my first objective was to take care of my health. That took me at least two years. Then, believe me, I never wasted a minute," Shyamal said.

He described becoming a tornado of activity: learning Indian vocal music, picking up the accordion again—something he hadn't done in years. He started studying art at exhibitions, which piqued his interest enough that he began commissioning the paintings now on the walls of his flat.

"From that point of view, I fulfilled some of my goals coming out of the money-hunting days in America," Shyamal said. "But the worst part was I remember the day I got on the plane. I cried for both of you. Every day, I used to pray. My first prayer was, 'God, protect my two children.'" He paused a beat before continuing. "I really meant it. How Sopan looks at me now—that was my concern. And yet, when I saw you, a spark went through my body.

Good thing you did, by coming. So I have some fulfillment. Some sadness in my life. But I am a strong believer in God. And both of you met my expectations."

"So you're religious," I said. *How does someone who dealt with such a difficult life still believe?* I wondered.

"No," Shyamal said.

"You just said you're a strong believer in God," I said.

"God and religion are two different things," Shyamal answered. "Religion is made by human beings. God is God. Who is God? Nobody knows. Studying science, cosmology, the origin of human beings, and seeing the huge cosmos, it's not possible that it is nature. There must be somebody, a supreme power."

My father's conception of God was really whatever you wanted it to be. He said that at any stage of life, one must believe in something. Work might be your deity in one stage, something else in another.

"In my case, yes, there's God," Shyamal said, pointing to his heart. "God is here."

Shyamal and I had stumbled on something else we shared: our agnosticism. I've always been skeptical of organized religion. Heck, I've always been skeptical that there are any higher beings at all. What God would saddle my parents with this kind of life? Not to mention the millions who face worse fates. Skepticism isn't wholesale rejection, though, and I'm with Shyamal here: This universe is too lush, too vast, and too wondrous for there not to be somebody pulling the strings. And in my darkest days, I've prayed, especially when I've felt helpless and needed the boost from someone (or something). Is that a lazy, convenient way of believing in a higher being? Welcome to agnosticism, where our Sunday sermons are just a bunch of us saying, "Eh?"

I imagine that my father has prayed way more than I have.

Assuming that we really are alike when it comes to this and how much of his life was seemingly out of control, he must have needed to ask for more.

Shyamal was not a resentful agnostic, but he certainly had to be bitter about how some aspects of his life had turned out, especially his marriage to Bishakha and what he viewed as the lack of support from his family growing up. Right? I wasn't so sure.

"Knowing what you know now, do you wish you picked a different way to get married?" I asked. "Regret," as I learned here, was as foreign a word for my father as "choice" was.

"Marriage is something else. Don't mix it up. Think of your case. Did anybody do a calculation for you that you would meet Wesley someday?" Shyamal said. "It just so happened. Wesley, in a short period of time, she impressed everybody in the family. But it so happened that you met and loved each other. It so happened that your love went deeper and deeper every day. Why? Dependence on each other. In my case, it never happened."

But Shyamal didn't think about regret in the way that I did, in that he didn't think about it at all. I, on the other hand, have always replayed life decisions in my head, wondering if I made the right choice, lamenting when one led to a negative outcome. Even though my parents' marriage was a failure, like many things in his life, Shyamal accepted it and didn't dwell on the past.

"I'm an engineer. Could I be better off in the medical science or as a musician? I don't know. Could be worse. Could be better. Marriage is like that," Shyamal said.

"Do you wish that you had the chance to meet someone in the way that I met Wesley?" I asked.

Shyamal dismissed it out of hand. "There are people who have dated for five years who can't survive marriage for one year," he said.

I could see Wesley out of the corner of my eye. Of course, my father was right in a way. Wesley and I could connect right now and then disconnect emotionally years down the road. Even months.

But still, Wesley and I being together wasn't as simple as picking a profession, as Shyamal analogized, or a matter of simple good luck (although there was certainly some of that). And contrary to what Shyamal said, it's not as black and white as simply ending up with the right or wrong person. Wesley and I had taken the time to sincerely pursue each other. It took work and vulnerability. We chose to be together in a way my parents never had the opportunity to. And if we do drift apart for some reason, it will also be a choice to do so. Jobs don't love you back in the way a significant other does. A long-term intimate connection has higher stakes compared to your career. One pays the bills. One keeps you warm.

I pressed on.

"Let me ask it this way. Given your history, do you resent the institution of arranged marriage?" I said.

"No, not at all."

"You never thought about remarrying?" I asked.

"No, no, no, no, no. So many girls have approached me as of now," Shyamal said.

My mind did a backflip. "Afterward, you mean?" I said, incredulously.

"Yes!" Shyamal said, clarifying that he meant in the last eleven years, not when he was with my mother.

"And you never considered it?" I said.

"No!" Shyamal let out another one of his high-pitched squeals.

"Why?!" This time I let out one of my own. He lived by himself in his old age. Finding companionship seemed like an ideal solution to me. In America, divorced parents remarry all the time.

Repeatedly, Shyamal said he had no regrets. About marrying Bishakha. About not remarrying. Really, about anything. It's just not something he could conceive of. Life happens, and then you move on. But he did admit that he once briefly entertained the possibility of remarrying.

There was once a "very pretty" Bengali woman from New Zealand who moved to India three years prior and had "many good qualities."

"She came here and sat down and talked to me," Shyamal said.

"About getting married?" I asked.

The two had been connected by the woman's relative, who happened to know him, and there was some courtship. My father said he played the accordion for her and that they occasionally went on dates together. He said that he brought her back to his house. This house. The woman was impressed by Shyamal's paintings on the wall and their conversations, he said.

I was in disbelief. I had never really discussed dating with my father before. I didn't count him meeting Bishakha as a date.

"What's wrong with that?" he said, noticing my writhing face.

I stammered that nothing was wrong and immediately steered the conversation toward more specifics about the mystery woman. She had an extra sense about my father. According to Shyamal, she suggested he would get bored by her. Shyamal agreed. After about six meetings over the course of a month, the two broke it off. My father was back on the singles boat.

Shyamal attributed his loneliness to being picky and demanding of those he surrounds himself with, but I see it differently and I'm betting the woman did too: He can be an impatient, rigid man and a challenge to live with.

"Getting a partner for me was always difficult," Shyamal said.

"So do you think there's an equal chance of being happy in an arranged marriage as in a love marriage?" Wesley tried her hand at getting my father to engage on a specific topic.

But again, my father demurred. "Marriage is luck," he said. "Marriage is luck."

Before we left for the night, Shyamal insisted I play his piano one more time. He set up a tripod and a camera to shoot my short performance. I sang an out-of-tune version of one of my favorite Billy Joel songs, "Summer, Highland Falls," and plinked some jazz tunes I knew. The Joel song, about manic depression, is one I've played since I was a child.

My father kept flashing the thumbs-up sign to show his approval. In some ways, the visit had come full circle. Sitting down at his piano was one of the first things Shyamal had me do when we initially arrived in Kolkata. Just like last time, I was playing a Billy Joel song. The Omar Sharif picture still hung nearby. But my father and I barely resembled the men who had reunited at the Kolkata airport. After traversing so much emotional ground, the same ground had shifted beneath us.

"Fantastic, very good. I appreciate it. Very proud of you," Shyamal said, clapping his hands.

Wesley and I packed up our belongings and got ready to head back to the hotel for the last time. We would be heading to Bengaluru shortly for Manvi's wedding, before meeting Shyamal again in Delhi.

My father's flat had its own cozy charm, infused with his personality, but it was missing something. I gave him a gift: a print of my first-ever front-page story in the *New York Times*, over which he gushed with joy. It was from the day of Trump's inauguration, which I helped cover during my first month on the job. The print would fit on his wall just fine next to his historically accurate paintings: The article had been rigorously fact-checked.

"Beautiful! Beautiful! Oh my god," Shyamal said, holding it in his hands. He leaned over and kissed me on the head. "You know, some of the writings I don't understand. I am not a man of literature. I am a man of engineering. But I read this with pride. So beautiful. My son."

Shyamal examined his wall for a place to hang the print. A driver was outside waiting to take us back to our hotel.

"This feels like home to you," I said, looking around. "This whole place. India. Kolkata. It feels like it's your home. Does it feel like home to you?"

Shyamal sighed.

"Yes and no," he said. "The lights of my life are not around me. You and Sattik. That does not make this home. That will never make this home."

His eyes darted to the *Times* print he clutched, then to our faces. My father, who claimed himself to be a man of no regrets, flashed a hint of sadness in his face. His lips pursed. Shyamal contemplated for a few seconds, before raising his head and fixing his stare on us again.

"But I am comfortable here," my father said.

Wesley and I left Shyamal's flat and climbed into the car. As we pulled away, my head swiveled toward his flat, cementing it in my mind. When we had first pulled up to this building, I felt I was nervously chatting with a stranger and was unsure of what to expect. Now I felt the sharp pain of a new normal.

THIRTEEN

"You've brought me everything."

Imagine, if you will, that you take a highly anticipated trip to a foreign country rich with diverse culture and history. You arrive at one of the five cities on your schedule. It's filled with endless sights to see and you have only a limited amount of time to see them. And you won't be back anytime soon, certainly not for several years.

Do you, on your only free day . . .

a. Wake up and immediately head out to start checking items off your sightseeing itinerary.
b. Wait, what about the local cuisine? Okay, eat breakfast and then consult the itinerary.
c. Since you're spontaneous, you roam the area without any plan in mind. Let the adventures come where they may.
d. Stay inside all day to binge-watch Season 3 of *The Americans*.

If you picked options A, B, or C, congratulations. You are a well-adjusted human being with a curiosity for the world around you. Wesley and I went with D.

Since Manvi's wedding itinerary skipped a day in the middle, we were free to explore Bengaluru, a city located in the southern part of India, which is known as the country's tech capital. But being in India's Silicon Valley wasn't enough to get me out of bed. I was emotionally and physically drained from almost a week with Shyamal, and these few days would serve as a much-needed intermission before seeing him again in Delhi after the wedding.

Even still, I honestly can't think of a worse way to embrace my Indian heritage than by spending a full day in India watching *The Americans*. But there we were. I didn't want to move. I didn't want to think. I didn't want to be plugged in. The only thing I wanted to be plugged in was the laptop, so we could watch more episodes. Shyamal's car crash, which I had only just learned was the impetus for him leaving the country, hung like smog in my brain.

That night, over dinner—at one of the hotel restaurants, of course—Wesley and I felt refreshed enough to relive the past week.

"It was clear from my dad that he puts zero blame on himself," I mused. "He's quite comfortable with how he was as a dad."

"Better dad than he had," Wesley said.

"He said, 'What more could I have done?' And it's tough to answer that question in the moment," I responded. "And the truth is, I don't know the answer to that question, but it doesn't feel like he was 100 percent father of the year."

I was conflicted. I understood a lot more about my father and his motivations. I appreciated the struggles he went through and saw the reasons for his shortcomings. But there was another part of me still deeply frustrated with him.

"I think it's less about things he could have done," Wesley

said. "It's more about an interest in your humanity that I don't think he quite conceptualizes. He would respond and say, 'I came to your plays, I came to your chorus concerts.'"

"Okay, but that opens up the question of was it even possible for him, given the cultural divide?" I said. I considered that even if my parents had been a good match, that Shyamal and I would still not have been close.

"And the answer is probably no, and so maybe what more he could have done is something that is not necessarily within his capacity," Wesley offered. "The answer could definitely be that he was the best dad he had the capacity to be, and it was not enough."

"I just don't think you go through your entire life being alienated from your children and you did nothing wrong," I said.

There was some bitterness that hadn't subsided. Maybe it would never leave. We paid the check and headed back to our room, where iTunes was waiting.

Wesley yelled from across the room: "Want to set up *The Americans*?"

The first part of Manvi's wedding celebration had been the prewedding *sangeet*, basically a night of performances from close friends and family. There were poems, dances (including a choreographed flash mob), singing, toasts, and, of course, gratuitous eating. A *sangeet* can last for days, although that is increasingly uncommon. Perhaps as karmic punishment for wasting so much time in India watching American (Russian?) television, on the day of the *sangeet*, I came down with crippling food poisoning as the result of some not-so-thoroughly cooked meat I ate the night before. There was no gratuitous eating for me, though the sight of me doubled over in pain probably just looked like a new twist on the Electric Slide.

I was thrilled to see Manvi and even more grateful to her for providing the nudge I needed to take this trip. Trying to have an extended conversation with the bride was like trying to get a question in at a presidential press conference. Each time she attempted an escape from the crowd to say hello to us, she found herself swarmed seconds later by an inexhaustible stream of family members. She and Jayanth, her soon-to-be husband, did get to meet Wesley, and we all hung out briefly by the bar. We had both come a long way since our days of improv.

On Day 3, the wedding ceremony began early in the morning. Have you ever been to an elaborate Indian wedding in the summer? It's like Coachella, but with higher temperatures and fewer drugs. The ceremony lasted approximately six hours and began with a procession of wedding guests being led into an open-air venue by a man playing a large drumlike instrument called a *thavil* and another one blowing a *nadaswaram*, a classical Indian reed instrument. Once inside, the resplendent colors being worn by the couple were visible even from across the room. They sat in the center with a priest, while the guests sat in bleacher seats on the outskirts of the pavilion.

When I say Coachella, I also mean in terms of attention span. At a concert festival, you might take some time at one stage, linger for a bit, and go to another one. You might not even pay attention to the act onstage. You might come late in the day or leave early. At this ceremony, guests lingered around the edge of a mammoth tent that was erected on the grounds of a picturesque venue about forty-five minutes away from the downtown area. Most were chatting during the ceremony, only paying attention intermittently to its many phases. Even the parents of the bride and groom circled the tent, mingling with guests to make sure they were comfortable.

I met several of Manvi's friends, whose lives seemed like the opposite of mine: Most of them were brought up in India, went to school in the United States, and returned to India as quickly as they could or were making eventual plans to do so. Many of our conversations swung back to them wanting to be with the family they had grown up with. It was of paramount importance for them to be home. I didn't really have much to offer on that front.

After an extravagant wedding reception at a downtown Bengaluru hotel, Wesley and I boarded a flight the next morning to Delhi, where we linked up with Shyamal for the last part of the trip.

Our first day in Delhi was, by far, our busiest, and it was a rainy one no less. Remember when I said my father had planned every facet of our final stretch? He had mapped out six sights for us to see that day, a mixture of architectural wonders and ancient sights that were his personal favorites. There was the stunning Lotus Temple, one of eight or so continental Bahá'í faith temples around the world; it was built in the shape of an actual lotus flower. The Bahá'í faith is particularly fascinating because it accepts all faiths as having validity, which seems to me to be an obvious path to world peace.

Shyamal took us to a local market, where Wesley bought some jewelry and pashminas. In some parts of India, gemstones are much cheaper than they are in America, partially because of the abundance of mines there, so Delhi was an ideal place to buy gifts for relatives at home. Wesley sat in a back room examining rubies with a magnifying glass, asking what I thought. I thought the air-conditioning and my cup of chai were great.

We also went to Purana Qila, a sixteenth-century fort. It has another common name: "Old Fort." The country responsible for beautiful names like Priyanka and Shivani somehow let a sight rich with history be nicknamed "Old Fort." It's like calling the place where the leader of your country lives the White H— Ah. Nevermind.

Many of the structures within the Old Fort were attributed to Emperor Humayun, the second Mughal ruler of India. We also went to the Red Fort, another Mughal structure, this one built by Shah Jahan, the fifth Mughal ruler. Its walls are made of red sandstone, hence its name. My father had done a lot of studying of the Mughal empire, the Muslim dynasty that led India for two centuries, and he excitedly imparted every bit of knowledge as often as he could. And when he wasn't teaching, Shyamal would randomly blurt out "THE MUGHALS!" like they were invading and he was the only one who saw them. Or we'd turn and look at him and we'd hear him mutter, "Old Fort!" and nothing else.

And once again, my father did that thing where he'd take pictures of us with his point-and-shoot camera without knowing how to use the zoom. So Wesley and I stood there, grinning for minutes, as he stepped forward and backward and then forward again until he got the composition he wanted. And then Wesley would hand him our smartphone to take another picture.

"BEAUTIFUL. I admire this camera so much," Shyamal would say.

We offered to send him our higher resolution pictures. But he wanted his own, so we indulged him and stood like mannequins whenever he asked. I only reached my breaking point once. At the last fort of the day, we stood for a few minutes, sticky and fatigued, while he snapped pictures. Then he spotted a bush nearby. Could we go stand behind the bush? No, Dad. Absolutely not.

I'll say this about Shyamal: His energy was impressive. At the end of the day, Wesley and I were nearly dead and drenched, a combination of sweat and rain. But Shyamal, armed with the spirit of THE MUGHALS, wanted to keep taking us to sights.

"I know you are tired. I'm tired also. But we will never get this day back," Shyamal said to Wesley and me.

The next day, we took a four-hour drive to Agra to see the crown jewel of the trip: the Taj Mahal. Shyamal told me that he had seen the Taj Mahal four times previously, the first time in

1965, when he came to Delhi for a job interview and took the train to Agra.

We caught our first glimpse of the world's most famous mausoleum from a highway in Agra. From there, the edges of its marble pillars and the top of its dome came to life like a storybook image.

"Holy shit. It's right there," I said.

I kept repeating myself.

"Holy shit. It's right there. Holy shit. It's right there. IT'S RIGHT THERE."

Anyone who has studied the Taj Mahal knows that it was built by Shah Jahan, who ruled India from roughly 1628 to 1658, as a tribute to his wife, Mumtaz Mahal, who died in 1631 while giving birth to the couple's fourteenth child. A grief-stricken Jahan wanted to make a romantic gesture, so he commissioned this grand tomb. It remains, to this day, the biggest romantic gesture in history.

What is less known is the Agra Fort, two kilometers farther up the Yamuna River, which Jahan renovated. It is where he was imprisoned at the end of his life by his son, Aurangzeb.

In 1657, Jahan became ill, setting off a bloody battle for a successor among four of his sons. Aurangzeb, the third oldest, emerged victorious. He executed two of his brothers, and the other fled the country. Aurangzeb placed his father under house arrest at the Agra Fort, where he remained until his death in 1666. The only view he had of the outside world for the last years of his life was that of his beloved monument to Mumtaz: the nearby Taj, where his remains would also be placed. Good thing he didn't just go with flowers.

This was what Shyamal most wanted us to see: Jahan's view from his prison cell. From this vantage point, one can see how much the Taj towers over Agra. In the distance are the outlines of residential areas and other buildings. But its immediate surroundings are all open fields. As I peered through a grated opening to see this more distant perspective, I wondered what Jahan must have thought seeing only this wonder in his waning days.

It wasn't until early the next morning that we got to tour the grounds of the actual Taj Mahal. Due to increasing pollution, cars aren't allowed near the complex, because petrol fumes had begun yellowing some of the marble. The closest we were able to get was about a mile from the Taj before walking the rest of the way. Once you arrive at the complex, you enter through a tunnel. The Taj is on the other side: a light at the end of the tunnel, somewhat appropriate for a tomb.

When we emerged, I let out a quiet gasp. Truly, this was the most awe-inspiring sight I had ever seen. The structure is an imposing and impeccably detailed work of art, looming over a reflecting pool with the tunnel on the other side. It was surprisingly peaceful. The day had just begun, so the area wasn't crawling with people yet, and the summer temperature wasn't oppressive.

Jahan was known for his love of design and architecture. The Taj was even more of a triumph if you consider how long it has been standing and the technologies involved in building it. In addition to the teardrop shape of the main building, which is accentuated by several columns of various sizes, Arabic inscriptions line the walls. The actual caskets of Mumtaz and Jahan are inside the structure. Even though the tomb was built for Mumtaz, Jahan's casket is in the center of the room and is bigger than his wife's.

Wesley and I toured the grounds by ourselves while Shyamal took pictures from afar. On the way back, merchants selling souvenirs accosted us left and right, recognizing us as tourists and easy marks. They competed with each other, each openly offering lower prices than their neighbor, although still higher than what they would normally charge, correctly assuming that we wouldn't know the difference.

Still marveling at the Taj, Wesley and I were open to buying some trinkets. Here we saw a side of Shyamal we hadn't seen yet: the haggler. The shops, essentially a line of stalls, were all located one next to the other. Each sold Taj-related merchandise: mini marble Taj Mahals. Taj Mahal plates. Taj Mahal postcards. Taj Mahal keychains. Taj Mahal candles.

My father insisted we leave any transactions to him, because he knew how this process worked. He deftly negotiated prices, even for tiny keepsakes, with each shop owner. Shyamal raised his voice and gesticulated wildly, throwing his arms wide, as he laid out the reasons each merchant was overcharging. And then he'd abruptly leave the stall midconversation and go to the next one to see if he could get a better deal. Sometimes the shop worker would chase after him and offer a lower price. Others would see if he was bluffing. But after fifteen minutes or so, it was clear Shyamal had a talent for this. He would've made the haggler in *Monty Python's Life of Brian* proud.

Shyamal wanted to send gifts back for Wesley's family. We told him that he could but to please keep it small, since we had so much to carry back with us to the United States. My father promised he wouldn't go overboard. We stood near the stalls, waiting for him to return.

"Overboard" is a relative term, apparently, because Shyamal came back with unwieldly bags, which held an ornate plate of considerable size (closer to a small platter) for Wesley's mother and a lamp for one of Wesley's brothers. *Dad, what did I just say?*

Shyamal insisted we'd be able to get all of this home with no problem. He just wanted to impress Wesley's family and thank them for bringing her into his life. I tried to protest, but there was no winning this battle. We were taking these gifts home, even if we had to throw some of our own clothes out to make it happen. *Fine.*

Agra is not a place you linger long after seeing the Taj, but my dad squeezed in one more stop at Fatehpur Sikri, about forty-five minutes away. We walked around the bright green pools at the Panch Mahal, quickly skipped barefoot across the hot marble at the Jama Mosque, then ditched Agra for the next stop on the Golden Triangle: Jaipur.

Jaipur would be our last stop before one quick night in Delhi to catch our flight home. I had blinked and we were already near the end of our trip.

The four-hour drive was a sleepy one. Shyamal napped in the front seat while Wesley and I watched more of *The Americans* in the back. We were hurtling down a mostly empty highway, a smattering of shops decorating the shoulder in some places and large herds of goats in others. I hate long drives. Like, really hate them. But I don't really like walking either, so traveling by car is the better option. It's a conundrum of lazy.

Out of nowhere, the tires screeched as our driver slammed on the brakes and swerved to the left.

There was a loud "*Moooooo!!!*" as the hindquarters of a cow smashed into our front bumper and up toward the hood of the car. Why did the cow cross the road? Well, he didn't really, because it was too late for our driver to stop. We crashed into the sacred animal at full speed, knocking it straight down.

The car stopped.

Thankfully, no one was hurt. Well, the car was hurt. The bumper was dislodged and the windshield cracked.

But a sense of panic quickly set in. *Forget the bumper! Check the cow!*

We had seen stray cows milling about, which didn't surprise us, since cows are sacred in India. I mean, you know that. Everyone knows that. Surrounding pedestrians don't really pay them any mind, especially because the vast majority of the population of India, roughly 80 percent, is Hindu. And since Narendra Modi became prime minister in 2014, cow lynchings, meaning the murder of human cow ranchers by vigilantes, have been on the rise. The majority of the states in India have laws that prohibit the killing of cows. That morning, just by chance, I happened to have read several articles about the subject. It had become a heated political issue in the country, an indication of rising sectarian tensions between Muslims and Hindus.

I was genuinely worried for our lives: Rajasthan, the state Jaipur is in, is one of those states which has a cow protection law.

People started emerging from the shops on the side of the highway to see what the fuss was about. I started breathing hard, mostly because, in the Indian criminal justice system, cows are represented by two separate yet equally important groups: gods and other gods. My father, meanwhile, didn't seem the least bit concerned. Mostly, he seemed annoyed that he had been awoken from his nap by this cow who had the misfortune of jaywalking at the wrong time. I was this close to saying we should make a run for it, but I knew I would make a terrible fugitive. I used to pretend I was a lampshade when I played hide-and-seek, even if we were outdoors.

Miraculously, the cow got up on its own and ran away, seemingly unaffected. And we—after a couple of minutes of staring imminent death in the face—started driving again, although with a dislodged bumper and cracked windshield. Newton was right: Every action does have an equal and opposite reaction. My heart was beating too fast. I tried to get myself together in the car by taking deep breaths.

As Shyamal prepared to take another nap, he pointed his finger to the left side of the road: "Oh, look at this store selling marble sculptures over there."

He then nodded off to sleep again. I threw my hands up in bewilderment. Was I the only one who realized the danger we had just escaped?

We made it to Jaipur without further incident, but our excitement for this leg of the trip was dampened knowing that it would be the last. There was no way around the fact that our stay in Jaipur was deeply sad. It had a different air than our other locations, even though, once again, we were touring palaces and forts.

I had been heartened in Kolkata to see my father so unexpectedly healthy and vibrant. I enjoyed pretending to play tennis with him and seeing his energy as a tourist, not to mention the sense of enlightenment I felt getting to know who he was as a person. But in the last couple of days before leaving for the United States, I was entirely filled with remorse.

Shyamal was a fussy traveler who didn't like deviating from well-laid itineraries. It occurred to me that this was probably because he rarely had other people with whom to travel, so he liked to retain as much control as possible. Siddhartha, his youngest brother, told me that the two of them don't tour together because they're too different. It sounded like something I'd say about my father.

By Shyamal's own admission, he had no friends in India. And it's not like he had lost many. In almost eight decades, he never made them. Once a day in Jaipur, Shyamal would say, "This has been a dream for you to come here." Or he'd be geeked about explaining the significance of a sight and say to Wesley, "I hope

I'm not boring you."

Sometimes the conversations exposed my father's deep loneliness. While he was never looking for sympathy, Shyamal would matter-of-factly make throwaway statements alluding to his lack of companionship that would prompt Wesley and me to exchange glances.

The most striking example was during lunch on the complex of another fort—this one called Nahargarh, one of our first stops in the city. It was a bit more difficult to get to, since it required driving on winding roads through the Aravalli mountains. But once we arrived, there was an extraordinary, sweeping view of the entirety of Jaipur.

He spent the meal quizzing Wesley on her career, joking that the key to life is avoiding tigers and lawyers. Wesley had dated me long enough to master the polite laugh.

"If you get time, come here during the winter and stay here for one night. It is a heavenly pleasure," Shyamal said, as we sipped beers.

"You didn't eat at this restaurant, did you?" I said, asking about his previous trips.

"This is the place!" he exclaimed.

Shyamal told us when he had been to this exact restaurant before: on New Year's Eve five years prior. He had come with a tour group. Me? I was surrounded by friends at a party at the same time. He also mentioned offhand that this trip to Delhi, Agra, and Jaipur was one of the only times in his life that he had traveled with someone who wasn't a stranger. He looked out the window as he said it. There was no fluctuation in his tone. He wasn't fishing for my comfort. This was his life. It was what he was used to.

"Believe me or not, I never expected in this short period of time to become so family. Both of you are my best friends,"

Shyamal said, and we clinked our beer glasses together. He said he was proud of me and that he was having the print of my front-page piece in the *Times* framed.

On our last day in Jaipur, we went to another shop, which sold everything from pashminas, rugs, and saris, to marble and wood carvings. We asked my father if we could buy him something for his kindness.

"You've brought me everything," he responded.

"What?" I said, confused.

"Everything I've lost in the last eleven years, you've brought me back in ten days," Shyamal said.

I said nothing, not knowing what I could add. I briefly thought about hugging him but decided against it. Instead, I helped Shyamal learn how to use his smartphone correctly. This way, the next time he was on a trip by himself, he could take photos with his phone rather than sprinting back and forth like Usain Bolt to get the perfect crop. My entire life, I had blamed Shyamal for not being able to properly communicate with me. This time, I was the one unable to communicate how much solace I found in getting to know him on this trip.

At the hotel the night before, Wesley had made an observation that I kept thinking about now, sitting across from my father: "He wants to know you but he doesn't know how to know another person," she had said. Maybe the opposite had been true as well. Maybe it was me who had not learned how to know him. That's not to assign blame. It may have just been that our respective places in the universe had been incompatible, and there is nothing we could have done about it until now. This particular intersection of time and place, both of us in a new stage of our lives, may have been the cipher we needed to find each other.

At the shop, we paid for our souvenirs, including a pashmina and some figurines to bring back for Bishakha, and then we got in the car for the drive back to Delhi. Shyamal was going to fly back to Kolkata the next day, Wesley and I to the United States.

The ride was quiet, except for one time when we pulled over. We didn't seriously injure a cow this time; it was just to have lunch.

"This time it'll be harder to say goodbye. Parting will be difficult," Shyamal said, as we munched on dosas in a crowded cafeteria.

After a couple of seconds of silence, Wesley offered, "It'll be weird to go home."

"At least you have each other. I go back to being alone," Shyamal said.

He paused and gazed off into the distance.

"It is hard to live alone," he said.

I'll never forget the unsentimental way he said this, his pure and unbridled resignation to a solitary life. He said it out loud, but really, it was to nobody in particular. The last couple of weeks were a break for Shyamal from his regular life, one that he'd treasure. His life would be lonely now. It would be here, it would be localized, and yet it would be so far away.

The next day, on the ride to the airport, Shyamal had on his white baseball cap, the same one he wore when we played tennis. He had a box in his lap, a painting from Jaipur he'd bought at a discount. We pulled up to a terminal, and I heard a deep sigh from Shyamal.

"Is this you, Dad?" I said.

"Yes," Shyamal said.

The driver found a parking spot on the sidewalk to unload my father's bags. There were honks and whistles surrounding us, just as there were in Kolkata when we had landed weeks earlier.

When he was all set, I turned to him and said, "Okay, Dad."

"Young man," Shyamal said, as we both went in for a hug. It was our first full embrace since I was in college. When we'd landed in India, he offered an awkward side hug and a tap on the head. But now he patted me on the back three times and kissed me on the cheek. Then he slapped me twice more for good measure.

He turned to Wesley with an exaggerated, "And?"

She came in for a hug of her own. "My sweetie," Shyamal said, kissing Wesley on the head.

We had the driver take a picture of the three of us. There was a part of me that hoped he would be a version of my dad and would take the picture like my iPhone was a point-and-shoot, so that the moment would last an hour instead of a second. Unfortunately, the driver knew how to operate a zoom lens.

We had to go to our terminal. Shyamal, not one for deep emotions, forced a grin, but I could see he was trying to hide his sadness. I could see the longing etched in the wrinkles on his face. Me too, for that matter. It was back to real life for all of us.

"Okay, Dad. We'll talk to you when we land, okay? Safe flight," I said, giving him one more hug and climbing back into the car. Right before Shyamal headed inside, he smiled and performed an uncoordinated shimmy with his body. I have no idea what he was trying to do, but I appreciated it nonetheless.

"He can't stop smiling. Look at him," I muttered.

As the car started moving, I stared out the window. Wesley was crying.

"What a couple of weeks," I said to her.

"Are you okay?" she said.

"Yeah," I said. I took her hand and kissed it. "I have you with me."

FOURTEEN

"For me, I didn't have a choice."

Mom, why would you say something?" I asked Bishakha, dumbfounded, clutching the tiny box in my pocket.

Wesley, my mother, and I were sitting in my mother's bedroom in New Jersey several months after returning from India. Wesley and I were mostly recovered from our trip and had gotten back into our normal routine. In the weeks after we'd landed at Newark Airport, I faced questions about the trip from co-workers and friends, which I didn't know how to answer. There was no way to succinctly do so. I just kept saying, "It was not a relaxing trip" and left it at that, which was probably for the best. When colleagues ask you a question about vacation, they don't actually want to hear the details.

Bishakha had just returned from India as well. She'd had to sell property belonging to her mother, who died when I was in college. My grandmother on my mother's side was the only grandparent I had ever met, and it was when I was very young. I barely remember her.

Before Bishakha left for her first trip to India in a decade, I had a request for her.

Back when Wesley was picking out rubies and sapphires for her family in Delhi, she had said offhand to no one in particular, "These rubies would look good on a necklace. Or earrings. Or a ring."

I know nothing about jewelry. I never ever buy it. If I was to go buy earrings right now, it's more likely I come back with pushpins and not know the difference. But when Wesley said that, my ears perked up and I made a mental note.

Rubies. Ring. Got it.

Wesley wasn't subtly telling me to propose. She didn't even remember the comment. At least, she said she didn't remember. But I filed it away for proposal purposes. Anyone who was willing to run an emotional ultramarathon with me in the way Wesley did was a keeper.

So when Bishakha informed me she was going to India, I told her if she happened to come across rubies that were comparatively cheap, I would appreciate her bringing them back so I could put them on an engagement ring of some sort. My mother was *delighted*. It meant a lot to her that I would consult with her about something like a proposal. It was a far cry from our awkward exchange about the girl who had a crush on me in sixth grade. Bishakha, in a solemn tone, said she would do her best.

After she returned about three weeks later, Wesley and I drove down to see her. Within minutes of walking in her front door, Bishakha ushered us into her bedroom. She had an extra bounce in her step, even as her movements were hindered by the noticeable limp caused by years of standing on her feet as a retail worker. We could smell the curries that were cooking in the kitchen.

We sat on her bed as she pulled out several bags from her closet and began to present gifts she had purchased. She handed Wesley a hot pink lehenga with gold embroidery and a handbag. She handed me a jar of pickles. No, really. Indian pickles are amazing condiments and not easy to buy in Manhattan, so this wasn't as big a slight as you may think. As Wesley felt the cloth in her hand, I prepared to stroll back to the kitchen for lunch. Except my mother had one more gift.

Bishakha, while beaming, tossed me a small, ring-sized jewelry box—*with Wesley in the room.*

"Shambo, here's what you asked for."

Just to reiterate: I had asked Bishakha to buy some rubies for me. Rubies to be placed on an engagement ring. A ring I would use to eventually propose to Wesley. A proposal meant to be a surprise. Thankfully, Wesley was looking at the lehenga when my mother gave me the box. Bullet dodged. She was none the wiser.

Except a minute later, Bishakha said loudly, "Do those jewels work for you, Shambo?"

I froze. Wesley looked up. "What jewels?"

I closed my eyes and shook my head, grimacing slightly. I couldn't think of a lie to get out of this. "What?" I said. I tried to buy some time. I'm not a good liar.

"What did your mom just give you?" Wesley said, confused.

"*Mom, why would you say something?*" I said.

She froze. The confusion on her face turned to horror. Her palm hit her forehead. "Ohhhhhh."

Bishakha had never been proposed to in her life. She didn't understand that this was supposed to be a romantic surprise. She immediately became profusely apologetic. "Baba, I didn't know."

I softened my expression and I turned to Wesley. "Remember when we were in India and you said that the rubies would look good on a ring? Well, I noted you said that, so I had Mom grab some and bring one back for an engagement ring."

Wesley blinked, nodded, and immediately turned back to her gifts. She was expressionless. We didn't discuss it again. She knew that she wasn't supposed to know about the box. When I was ready to bring it up, she knew I would. My mother, however, repeatedly apologized for many days afterward.

I wasn't angry with her. In fact, I was astonished that she and I were at a point where we could openly discuss my significant other. It seems simple, perhaps inconsequential, but this isn't something that comes easy to some children of immigrant parents. That is especially true for a relationship as distant as ours had been.

There are two family outings with Shyamal and Bishakha that remain clear in my memory. They're memorable in large part because they were unusual for us. One, when I was about nine, was a trip to see *Titanic* in the theater. My parents enjoyed the movie, although it occurs to me that the reason I recall it all these years later is that it was the first time I saw nudity on the big screen, with my parents next to me no less, looking absolutely horrified.

The other was seeing the musical *Cats* on Broadway at the Winter Garden Theatre. I was probably around six. It was the only Broadway show that either of my parents ever saw because doing cultural excursions that were distinctly American—like going to see a Broadway show—was just not something my parents actively sought out. It was my first show as well, and I recall finding the costuming quite strange.

My parents were more interested in exposing me to Indian

culture. My mother enjoyed taking me to concerts featuring Indian classical musicians until the toxicity in the household became unbearable. I'd sit next to her in the audience and watch as she smacked her hands on her thighs along with the rhythms of the songs.

It was in the spirit of the *Cats* outing that I invited Bishakha to take a long bus ride so I could take her to see a Broadway musical. Now I could introduce my mother to cultural spaces in which I was interested. Since *Cats,* I've seen many shows, mostly because of my job at the *Times,* where I was writing about the stage fairly often for the culture section.

I knew she didn't know much about theater and that she didn't get to see live performances at all nowadays, but I predicted she would be amazed by the world-class voices and movement onstage. I also wanted to have the conversations with her like those I had with Shyamal in India. I figured seeing a show beforehand would ease any apprehension Bishakha had about discussing deeply buried issues.

But what show? The thing about Bishakha is that she's old-fashioned. Yes, she's more aware of pop culture than Shyamal. But she doesn't like vulgarity or violence. She loves family-friendly sitcoms, like *Full House* and *Everybody Loves Raymond.* I remember *Bonanza* reruns on TV Land being part of her television diet.

It shouldn't have been too hard to find a musical that would've been ideal for her. After all, most popular Broadway shows are campy, safe for all ages, and have a happy ending. Think of *42nd Street* or *The Lion King.* But maybe it was the comic in me, craving to find the humor in every situation like getting blood from a stone. I asked my mother if she wanted to see a Sunday matinee of *Chicago,* the dark, raunchy revival about sex and murder. I told her Cuba Gooding Jr. was one of the leads, and since Bishakha knew who he was, she said yes. It would be her second Broadway show and we had great seats, eight rows from the front. I didn't know if she would like it. A musical with an antihero named Roxie Hart at the center?

As we settled into the orchestra section, I could see Bishakha's eyes traveling around the theater as audience members filed in. Once the house lights came down and the curtain rose, she sat up slightly and I could see the corners of her lip turn upward. Gooding Jr. came onstage in character as Billy Flynn and yelled, "Is everybody ready? Is everybody here? *Hit it!*" Bishakha was wearing a broad smile as he broke into his big number "All I Care About." He has that effect on people.

She didn't like this show: *She loved it*. The murder scenes. The dancing. The singing. Cuba. She was *into it*.

"Baba, I've never seen anything like this. Wow," she said to me during intermission. Every now and then, when I glanced over at her, she would have her chin resting in one palm, a slight grin on her face. Sometimes she'd pat her thighs along with the show tunes, just as she used to at the Indian concerts we went to in my youth. It was perhaps silly of me to assume she wouldn't appreciate exceptional theater, but much of this journey had involved false assumptions.

After the final bows, we walked eight blocks back to my apartment, where Wesley was making dinner. We sat at the kitchen counter and began talking. As they had with Shyamal, the conversations lasted for hours and were startlingly honest and painful. But maybe because I had already gone through this with my father—and we both really enjoyed *Chicago* a few hours before—the exploration felt much smoother. I had more patience with her than I had Shyamal, and a bit less anger.

"I want to learn everything about you," I said to her. Once

again, I pressed a button on the voice recorder so it could begin recording. "I don't know where you were born. I don't know where you came from. I don't know how many family members you have."

"You ask me, I'll tell you. Your grandfather died when we were young."

I started with the same question that I asked my father: "When is your birthday?"

"My birthday is December 23, 1948. Actually, that was my passport birthday, but my real birthday is January 31, 1949." (In an odd coincidence, the birth date that had been falsely given Shyamal in childhood was Bishakha's actual date of birth, just four years apart.)

My mother's recollection of dates from several decades ago was not wholly sound, but she did her best. With my father, the birth date discrepancy was a purposeful decision to make his age more palatable for professional and academic advancement. With Bishakha, it was a case of shoddy paperwork stemming from her immigration into Canada from India.

"Because when I came to Canada, someone made a mistake on the passport," Bishakha explained. "We overlooked it. We didn't care. And then all of a sudden we noticed that it was a big gap in between. I went to India with that passport, and then I called and they said it would take a lot of paperwork. They said, 'Why don't you keep it the way it is?' I've been keeping it that way."

I imagine the dialogue with an immigration official: *Congratulations on your passport! And your new birthday!* What? *Your new birthday!* That's not my—*Yes, it is. Congratulations on your new birthday!* Okay, thanks.

Bishakha was born in Asansol, a city in West Bengal roughly 130 miles northwest of Kolkata. Her maiden name was Sarkar and she lived with her mother, Amiya, along with Amiya's father, an aunt, and an uncle. The city is known for its coal, steel, and textile plants. It's now a fairly developed city, but when my mother was growing up it was more rural than urban.

Her only brother, Atish, is about six years younger. He is someone whom we saw fairly often growing up. He immigrated to Canada too, although after my mother, and we usually made one trip a year to see his family in Toronto, where he still lives today. He is a cheerful, loving guy who provided one of the few truly warm familial interactions my brother and I had in our childhood.

Amiya was the only grandparent of mine I ever met. We'd see her when she was living in Toronto with Atish. My great-grandfather, Amiya's father, was a doctor. Pravat Kumar Sarkar, my grandfather, worked as a supervisor at a steel plant in Durgapur, a city thirty miles away from Asansol. That's where he lived as Bishakha grew up, but he visited Asansol often.

Bishakha said she was closer to Pravat than she was to her mother. They bonded over a mutual love of reading, which my mother described as his biggest passion. She said she used to have discussions with her father about the poetry of Alfred, Lord Tennyson and Henry Wadsworth Longfellow. My mother and I never discussed the specific content of books, but she did insist I read a lot of them. She used to make us take weekly trips to the library when I was growing up. She was more insistent on me reading than any other subject. (Although I don't think she intended for me to fall in love with the *Choose Your Own Adventure* series, as opposed to the rich works of, you know, the John Steinbeck types.)

"All kinds of books. It's not only the Bengali books," Bishakha said of her father. "He could tell you Shakespeare. He'd close his eyes and he could read that. He could tell you *Taming of the Shrew*.

He could tell you *Romeo and Juliet*."

Pravat may have been a quiet type, but my mother said he was also a "troublemaker." Before Pravat and Amiya were married, my grandfather used to take part in protests in support of Indian independence, activities that landed him in jail before my mother was born.

Amiya was a teacher, but Bishakha didn't know what subject she taught.

In Asansol, my mother attended a school run by missionaries, where her favorite subjects were history and literature.

My grandmother enrolled Bishakha in classical dance lessons, but my mother said she was mostly interested in burying her head in books.

"I didn't have very many friends," she recalled. This was something Bishakha had in common with Shyamal.

When she was about thirteen, my mother, Amiya, and Atish moved to Durgapur to be with my grandfather. Amiya quit her teaching job. About three years later, Pravat died suddenly of a heart attack while visiting Puri, a town that is the site of holy pilgrimages and known for its beautiful beaches.

"He died in front of everybody. I was not there, but my mother was there and others, like, my cousins. They were there."

Bishakha said she had remained behind in Durgapur to stay with an aunt and uncle. She found out Pravat died through a telegram. "We didn't believe it," she said. "I thought they were making fun out of it and joking. It was a really big shock for us. And then when they burned the body, then we realized, yes, he's gone. It was very bad, because he was the only earning member in the family."

Almost immediately, she told me, she went to Canada at Amiya's request.

"I came here first."

"By yourself?" I asked.

"Yes, they sent me by myself."

"Who sent you?"

"My mother."

"Why?"

Bishakha paused.

"Because Canada was like—remember, I have an uncle? My uncle didn't help me, but you met him."

"I don't remember."

"You don't remember. Okay. He was here, and then in India, it was a very bad situation. Very bad."

"You guys were not making money?" I asked.

"Not making money, plus political reasons. That they are killing everybody, you cannot go out. There was a lot of chaos going on in those days. There's a lot of problems going on in that situation. So they said, 'You come here.'"

This answer seemed a bit strange to me, but I ignored my instinct that something was being left out. From what I could tell of what Bishakha was saying: She had an uncle who was already living in Canada when Pravat died, who helped (or didn't help) facilitate her emigration from India. Amiya, Bishakha's mother, sent her to Canada to start a new life for herself. She was about sixteen years old and was sent to a foreign country where she didn't know the language and barely knew anybody, almost immediately after her father unexpectedly passed away, someone to whom she was close. My mother hadn't even been on a plane before.

"What did you think about coming here? Did you want to come?"

"I was very young, I didn't even know what was going on."

"But you were sixteen," I pushed. Something about this didn't sit right with me.

"Still, in those days, sixteen, you were too immature."

"But you didn't have a say," I kept prodding.

"I didn't have anything to say. No, no, no, no, no."

My mother saying "No" repeatedly reminded me of Shyamal.

"You couldn't say, 'No, I don't want to go,'" I said.

"No. I didn't even know what was going on!" Bishakha exclaimed. She was talking about this as if she was duped.

How could my grandmother essentially exile Bishakha away from her home? What mother could do that to her child with barely any discussion? Had Amiya packed Bishakha's bags and put her on a jet? Just like that?

When Bishakha first arrived in Toronto, she lived with a family friend and began attending high school, then community college. But she was also tremendously (and understandably) homesick. Bishakha didn't like the food in Canada. She didn't know how to cook for herself. She missed Bengali books and her favorite curries at home. My mother said she cried a lot.

Of course she did. Who wouldn't at that age, after what had happened? Three years after she arrived, from her telling, Amiya and Atish moved to Canada as well. Bishakha sponsored them. Atish was about thirteen.

"Ma didn't want to go back, so I got stuck here. If they wanted to go back, I could've gone," Bishakha said, barely hiding her regret. Incidentally, when I was growing up, Amiya did go back to India, which is why I only met her a handful of times.

When her family arrived, my mother stopped going to classes at the community college and took a job at nights as a switchboard operator at the Bell Telephone Company. She had to work to support Amiya and Atish on her own. And then over the years came other odd jobs, including a part-time gig at a library.

"When you were young, what did you want to do when you grew up?" I asked.

"You know what? I never thought what I wanted to be," she responded. "Because I didn't have time to think about me. Now I think a lot." Every word seemed to be dripping with sorrow.

"So when you're growing up, even when you weren't busy, you never had thought, 'Oh, I want to be an astronaut when I grow up?'"

"I didn't have time."

She wasn't comprehending what I was asking. She knew what the words meant, but not the meaning of the question. Once again, this reminded me of the conversations I had with Shyamal. Choice, the concept of agency, was so foreign to both of them.

"Did your parents ever talk to you about marriage and who you were going to marry?"

"No. When I was growing up in India, you have to have degrees, right, and then they will arrange for your marriage. And the man's family background has to be good, and then you have to see the man, what kind of job he has, because they have to provide. They will check all those things."

"But I'm saying, your father and your mother never said, 'Okay, at this age we're going to arrange you off.' Did you ever have a discussion about that?" I asked. I kept following up, my journalistic nature to pry fully engaged.

"No. It's understood. It's going to happen."

"And you have no choice in the matter."

"For me, I didn't have a choice. I never even thought of that. It didn't cross my mind."

"Before you met Baba, was there ever anybody else that you were in love with or anything like that?"

Bishakha let out a laugh, the first I'd heard all day since *Chicago*. "Never."

Her brain just wasn't wired that way. Where I have spent years dedicating brain space to crafting the perfect way to ask someone out on a date or constructing the perfect cover letter for the next job, it never occurred to my mother to find a husband on her own or to think about pursuing her own goals. She never *had* her own goals. My mother just had to survive. I can't even comprehend what a burden that must have been.

Familial pressures controlled my parents' plights, but Bishakha had the *opposite* experience of Shyamal in leaving India. Shyamal *wanted* to do it, but his family forbade it. But for the first time in his life, as he told me, "The steering wheel was in my hand." So he had at least found he had the agency to take his fortune in his own hands, even if that meant alienating his family. My mother didn't *want* to come but was, essentially, shoved off to Canada at a young age. She was forced into what her family thought would be a better life, far away from what she considered home.

The steering wheel was nowhere near her hands. Bishakha faced a responsibility far beyond herself, having to keep Amiya and Atish afloat. This experience might speak to why they had such different approaches to life: My father left to go back to India because he was used to doing things his own way, even if it alienated those close to him. Maybe Bishakha didn't ever go back to India permanently because she didn't think she could.

Hearing about Bishakha's feelings of loneliness growing up in India, feelings that were then compounded by her move to Canada, put her marriage to Shyamal in a completely different light for me. What struck me wasn't so much that she didn't have many choices growing up and as a young adult. It was that it didn't occur to her to even think in those terms. Bishakha had spent her life as a human ping-pong ball, being batted through life by other people. In my head, I thought of a terrible analogy: a sheep raised in a farm solely to supply wool and then forced into the wild. In the moment, I couldn't help but feel a twinge of anger toward Amiya. How could a mother have put her daughter in that position?

And then came her marriage, which she also didn't want. Yet another major life decision that was not her own.

"When your mother answered the ad, did you know she was doing that for you?" I asked Bishakha.

"No."

"You didn't know?"

"No, I was a bit surprised. When your dad came, my mother called and said, 'Somebody came and would like to see you.' So then he called me at the office. I was really shocked. I didn't know who that guy was. He said, 'My name is So-and-so and your mother gave me the number and I'd like to meet you.' So I said, 'I don't know you. I don't want to meet you because I have to go home.' He said, 'So, that's okay, go home, then we can see you there and we can go out.' I didn't like it."

For the most part, aside from some details, Bishakha's story about how they met was the same as Shyamal's. They were both in sync on one particular detail.

"He was desperate!" my mother exclaimed. "He wanted to get married as soon as possible, which I didn't because I wanted to wait."

"Why did you want to wait?" I asked.

"I didn't know your dad!" she said. She said that before committing to marriage, she wanted Shyamal to meet other members of her extended family, like her aunts and uncles.

Bishakha described her first meeting with Shyamal as "not good" and said "it didn't go well." She smiled as she said that. My mother didn't like the way my father carried himself.

"You know your dad," Bishakha said. "He is very aggressive, and I'm aggressive. I think I'm aggressive but not in front of people. I cannot be that kind of aggressive. I was not interested in marrying him."

"Did you tell your mother that you didn't want to get married to him?"

"Oh yeah, I told my mother."

"So why did you end up getting married to him?"

"I didn't have a choice. I don't blame my mother, either. She was very sick. She was worried about me. She was in the hospital. She thought, 'If anything happens to me, who is going to take care of her?'"

I found this incongruous with my mother's story about being sent to Canada by herself, but I didn't press. Amiya wanted Bishakha looked after and cared for, and yet Bishakha was the one who was taking care of the family at the time. She was shouldering the burden so that Amiya and Atish wouldn't have to face their struggles alone. This was apparently too much for Amiya to bear.

My parents' wedding ceremony took place in Pearl River, New York, in 1977. They were married by a local priest in front of around fifty guests. My mother was in her late twenties at that point. She had been an immigrant for more than a decade.

"Are you angry that your mother made you get married to him in hindsight?" I asked.

"At the beginning, I was not angry," Bishakha said.

But as the tensions with my father set in right as the marriage began, Bishakha's resentment for Amiya grew. The end result of the wedding was ironic: Amiya urged Bishakha to enter into marriage so my mother wouldn't be alone. Decades later, she was.

FIFTEEN

"I am happy, yes and no."

A thought ran briefly through my head in my conversations with Shyamal and Bishakha: I wish I had never been born.

I don't mean that in the way it comes off. I'm very glad I was born. I love living and I've been afforded luxuries the vast majority of humans in the world don't enjoy. I've been in love. I've been heartbroken. I've been able to pursue my professional desires, then switch gears when I wanted. I didn't grow up poor. I've traveled to most of the United States and some of Europe.

What I mean is, I wish my parents hadn't met each other and had instead found different paths, the by-product of which would mean I wouldn't exist. I don't blame myself for my parents' marriage, of course. I saw that episode of *Mister Rogers' Neighborhood*. But after hearing their stories and realizing just how unfit they were to be with each other, I wanted to take a time machine to 1977 and beg them to meet other people. They deserved better. Better from their parents. Better from each other. And yes, better from me.

"Why did I have a second child?" my mother repeated the question with a blank expression.

We were still in our kitchen, as Wesley prepared a new lamb curry recipe. Unlike the conversation with Shyamal, Wesley didn't sit with us for this one. While she listened impassively, she felt it would be better if this talk was just between us. We were going to traverse sensitive material, and we didn't know how comfortable Bishakha would be if the conversation got too crowded.

Bishakha was about thirty when she had my older brother, Sattik, in 1979. When I was born in 1988, she was almost forty. That means both of my parents had more than a decade of misery together before deciding to bring me into the world. It also means my mother was older than usual to have a child.

I asked my mother the same question I did Shyamal in India: "Why did you have a second child?" When I examined this with Shyamal, he said, "I loved both of you in the deepest core of my heart. Life is not about mathematics. It can happen to anybody. When you came, I was very happy to see you." He added it was "hard to say" whether it was planned. He didn't understand the question.

"Why have me?" I repeated myself to my mother.

"You're my miracle baby. God blessed me with you," she said, adding that the pregnancy was a difficult one.

"But why have a second child? Do you know what I mean? I'm not disputing that I'm your miracle baby and all that, but why have—you're already in an unhappy marriage."

"It's very hard to say why. I cannot say why."

Shyamal had said the same thing: *hard to say.* In fact, he used those exact same words when I prodded him about whether I was a planned child or not.

"It's just because having another child is just a lot more work and you're already tired, you're already exhausted," I said, but my mother interrupted.

"I got help from your *dada*," she said. *Dada*, in this case, referred to my brother, Sattik. That's what I used to call him growing up, which is how one addresses an older brother in India as a show of respect. "He helped me a lot. I'm grateful to him. I'm thankful to him. He loved you so much then. He used to pray in front of God and say, 'I want my brother, I want my little brother.' I was not even pregnant then. And God listened and I never, never, never, not a single moment, think that I made a mistake."

"But you guys went out of your way to have a child," I said.

"It just happens."

"It just happened?"

"I cannot explain to you, it just happened after nine years."

I realize that my line of questioning might seem insensitive. These questions may not be easy for any parent to answer, and I was pushing, straining to find a justification for my existence that might not exist.

And that was as far as I was going to get down this path anyway, so I moved on. I was a bit frustrated. Sometimes things are truly unexplainable. Maybe my parents' marriage was experiencing a détente, and here I am.

"I don't regret, Shambo," Bishakha continued. "Never. I was so happy when I saw your face when you were born. I said, 'Thank God, he is beautiful.' You used to have beautiful hair, cuddly ears."

"I used to. I don't anymore," I quipped.

"You were chubby. You were eight pounds, six ounces. You never smiled."

For a moment, my mother thought about Shyamal. This was not someone she thought about often. She looked away. Once again, her chin rested on her palm.

"He's happy there, and I'm a survivor."

"You are a survivor, that's very true," I said. She was mistaken about my father being wholly happy in India. But she was right about being a survivor. She laughed.

"Thank God you got out good. I don't want anything from my life. I just want you and Bimbo to stay well." ("Bimbo" was my parents' nickname for Sattik. Poor guy. I got "Shambo." He got "Bimbo.")

I had another topic to broach with Bishakha. I saved it for the end, knowing it would be the most difficult. When we were in India, and I sat at Shyamal's kitchen table, I had one overarching question I needed to ask my father: Why did he leave the country without telling me? I wanted to know everything else about him, of course. But what I most needed an answer to, more than anything else, was why he chose to physically disconnect himself from me. It led to some of our most difficult conversations and some of the most revealing answers from my father.

With my mother, the subject gnawing at me the most regarded the last time Shyamal and Bishakha lived under the same roof. I had never asked my mother about what happened in eighth grade when we were in Howell—that extended period where she locked herself in her room unexpectedly, marking our first period of sharp disconnect. It set off a chain of events that permanently split our family apart, not that we were that united to begin with. We never mentioned it after she reemerged from her self-imposed isolation. Fifteen years later, one of us needed to bring it up.

"When I was in eighth grade, there was a point where you really struggled, I think," I said, hesitantly.

"Oh yeah," Bishakha said matter-of-factly.

"You didn't come out of your room at all, except to go to work. Occasionally you'd come out and eat something. We didn't talk almost that whole year."

"At one point, I was thinking about killing myself at that time," Bishakha said, again almost casually.

"I didn't know what was happening. I never knew," I said, as softly as I could.

"In that case, nothing really happened."

"I remember. It came out of nowhere," I said.

"Sometimes, that's the way it is. That's the way he was. I had never seen him in a good mood," Bishakha said, referring to Shyamal. According to my mother, years of not feeling loved at home had taken its toll.

"So there was never a day of happiness in your marriage?"

"No, never."

"There was never a trip you took? Never a dinner?"

She said no.

"What were you feeling like in your room? What would you be thinking about all day? Did you actually think about killing yourself at that point?"

"Oh yeah, so many times."

"Especially at that point?" I said, keeping my voice calm and steady.

"Especially at that time," Bishakha said. Her voice was beginning to crack.

"What was going through your head?"

"Lonely."

"You were lonely. Did you feel like nobody loved you?" I asked.

"Oh, very much."

It was a terrible thing to hear. She was living in her own house, surrounded by family, but feeling loved by none of them. During that period, she took my confusion as a lack of caring for her. This is what I mean by saying she deserved better from me.

Why didn't we just all talk to each other and say how we felt? It seems *so simple*. All I had to do was go upstairs and knock on her door. Maybe slip a note underneath and tell her that if she needed anything, I was there. But this didn't even *occur* to me. I was so focused on living my own life that I didn't consider that my *mother* needed me. Things would have been so much easier. We would've relieved each other of so many burdens if we had just taken all of our internal anguish and made it external. Here was Bishakha, a woman who had so much robbed from her and had never been in love before. Even now, I wondered when was the last time she felt true unconditional love. When her father was alive? Her childhood? My guilt was real. I swore in that moment to never let my mother feel alone again.

"Do you wish we communicated more growing up? Because we didn't really," I said.

"We should have, but maybe it's my fault, I don't know."

"This is not just your fault. This is not just Dad's fault. This is not just my fault. It's all of us," I said.

I felt strongly about that. In order for us to mend—*truly* mend the family fabric—we all had to accept collective responsibility.

"You're happier now?" I asked.

"I am happy, yes and no. I'm not happy. I'm not happy because I don't have a family. I'm by myself. I've survived. Whatever I'm doing, I'm doing okay. Yes, I think I'm happy."

"If you could do it over again, going back to when you were like eighteen?"

Bishakha laughed. It was true that she hadn't thought at the time about what kind of career she wanted, but it didn't mean she couldn't think of one now. She said she would have become a librarian.

"I definitely would not have listened to my mother about my

marriage."

"Would you have gone to college?"

"I would have done that."

My mother went on to say that her relationship with her mother became strained after she married Shyamal. In the late 1990s, Amiya had moved back to India. Shortly before her death, when I was in college, Bishakha went to see her one last time. Amiya knew she was dying, and their last conversation was very emotional.

"She cried and I cried," Bishakha said.

"Did your mother ever say anything to you like 'I'm sorry I made you marry him'?"

"No, but I'm sure she regrets it a lot. She did regret a lot," my mother said, before continuing: "In her mind, she knew she made a big mistake. But she did cry a lot. And she said, 'This is the last time you're going to see me.' And that's what happened. She died before the year's end."

Even still, Bishakha did not seem critical of the institution of arranged marriage, saying that she and my father were just "one in a hundred." For all their dissimilarities, this was one place where Bishakha and Shyamal saw eye to eye.

As we were talking, Bishakha noticed Wesley sitting in our living room, waiting while the curry simmered. She had been silent the whole time. My mother turned to her. "God gave me a good one. The best thing in my life, him," Bishakha said to Wesley, referring to me. "Everybody asks me, 'What is the best thing in your life?' I would say him. Even if I died right now, I would say my best thing in my life, him."

Bishakha, who was keenly aware I would not have picked up the phone to call her on Mother's Day last year without Wesley's prodding, was expressing her affection. She seemed resigned to the estrangement between herself and Sattik, which was cemented around the time of my college graduation, due in part to disputes over Sattik's wedding.

"I am ever grateful to you and thankful to you," she said to Wesley. "And if you ever get married, I am not going to interfere. I promise that."

I was done talking for the day. We had covered so much in a short time, and now I just wanted for us to enjoy each other's company. I turned the recorder off. If Bishakha felt relieved, she didn't show it in that moment.

Wesley's lamb curry was soon finished. I set out plates and scooped out helpings for the three of us before migrating to our tiny living room. My mother didn't eat much, but she did heap praise on Wesley's culinary skills. As we munched, I turned on the television and scrolled through various channels, trying to find something for us to watch. Perhaps a movie. Not *Chicago,* of course. I landed on the Pixar feature *Coco,* the animated story of a young boy who runs away from a restrictive home out of anger, ends up in the afterlife, and spends the film trying to get back home to his family. It was a little too on the nose, but it felt right nonetheless.

I couldn't tell if my mother enjoyed the movie. She leaned back against our couch cushions with her hands interlocked on her lap in front of her and was silent for most of it. Maybe she was at peace. After the movie ended, happy ending and all, we decided to call it a night.

The next morning, I took Bishakha to a Sprint store and purchased her first smartphone. She was still using the flip phone I bought for her from the mid-2000s and was overdue for an upgrade. I had flashbacks of teaching her how to use email, and I hoped this process would be quicker. This time, I'd have to teach her text messaging, emojis, apps and—gulp—social media. I cringed at the prospect of her calling and asking me to explain memes to her. But I started easy, selecting a basic Samsung, rather than the most up-to-date iPhone. Crawling before walking seemed appropriate.

On the sidewalk outside, I showed her basic functions as I walked her to the Port Authority bus that would take her back to New Jersey. *Here is how you call. Here is how you take pictures.* Lesson two would include “How to Retweet.” My mother beamed and thanked me. We embraced and then she headed home.

It felt like we were all getting an upgrade.

SIXTEEN

"There were stories I heard."

Bishakha handed Wesley and me a handwritten card in her New Jersey apartment two days before Christmas. It read: "Dear Wesley, you are my sun, the moon, and the stars. To Shambo, Merry Christmas." Shakespearean affection aside, Wesley and I had come to celebrate the holiday with her a few weeks after our kitchen table conversation. This wasn't something I had done in ten years or so.

We had arrived with gifts enough to make up for lost time: candles, fancy bath soaps, homemade fudge, and the crown jewel—a framed picture of the three of us. After she excitedly unwrapped them in her living room, my mother placed the frame on my childhood piano. It was the only picture in her apartment, but it felt like the start to a collection.

Bishakha seemed galvanized. One sign of this was the huge containers of Indian food she piled in our arms as we left a couple of hours later. I knew how much it meant to her to be able to cook for us.

In exchange, we gave her some more lessons on how to use her smartphone. That day's seminar was titled "How to Send a Text." It was the next logical step. Just like the email tutorial in college, it was a painstaking process. I'd take her phone, write a sample text, and give it back to her, and she would try to mimic what I did. This went on for a while, with minimal progress, and then Wesley and I had to go. I wasn't sure if she would be able to do it.

In the hours afterward, I ignored my phone while Wesley and I were driving to Sattik's house, where we would spend the rest of the holiday. When I finally checked it, I saw several text messages. All from one source: my mother, who had proven a quick learner.

Well, sort of. The first string of text messages went like this:

Hi
Hi Shsmbo
Thanks
Hi shambo
Hi shambo
Hi shambo thank you
[blurry picture of the living room floor]

She had some work to do to expand her texting repertoire—and learn to wait for answers!—but, then again, self-expression was never her strong suit.

That gift was inherited by her younger brother, Atish.

For many years during my childhood, Bishakha, Shyamal, Sattik, and I would climb into our car and make the almost ten-hour drive from New Jersey to Toronto to visit him. Greeting us as we exited the car like stiff, bedraggled nomads was the ever-smiling Atish, his wife, Sima, and their son, Sagnik, who is a couple of years younger than me.

The visits were the highlight of my year. They lasted about a week and usually took place during summer break or at Christmastime. Atish and Sima lived in a small apartment in the downtown area of the city, and I can still smell the carpeted lobby of their building: a damp leather combined with the chemical scent of a car air-freshener. Atish, whom we call "Munna Mama," is a portly, jovial man with a mustache and an enthusiasm that bristles with every sentence he utters. He never said, "Hey Shambo." It was, "HEY SHAMBO!" He always bought toys to spoil Sattik and me, everything from computer games to Pokémon cards.

Sima—or, as we call her, "Mami"—doted on us. I never felt nervous around her, as I did around other adults, including other members of my family. She was calm and steady, and her cooking was top-notch. Her best dish was a butter chicken we would beg her to whip up, even if she had just made it the night before.

Atish and Sima loved us, and we loved them. Even the socially awkward Shyamal looked forward to going north of the border. Whatever turmoil was going on at home seemed to dissipate during our Toronto visits, flushed out by a cold Canada chill and the warmth of Atish and Sima. Simply put, being around them wasn't stressful, and that wasn't something to take for granted when it came to our family. The most comfortable memories were of sitting around inside, a crucial element of Indian family gatherings. Brown family reunions usually aren't destination events. We don't go camping. There aren't fifty of us renting a cabin in the Poconos. We head to whomever has the closest living room.

My family preferred to squeeze in on Atish and Sima's couch, gabbing endlessly about anything and everything while sipping chai, rather than going out and experiencing the city. Sometimes my family would ask (er, command) me to sing a classical Indian song while playing the harmonium in the living room. Those were the moments where everybody fell silent, as I ran my fingers up and down a keyboardlike instrument about the size of small treasure chest. Bishakha and Sima would close their eyes and bob their heads back and forth as I sang.

When we *did* leave the apartment, we would do quintessential brown things. We'd go to Indian clothing stores, where saris adorned the windows, and Indian restaurants (when we didn't have an Indian dinner at home). In the evening, we'd go to the homes of other Indian family and friends, where we'd wear Indian clothing and eat more Indian food. At this point, I still felt my brownness. I liked the food. I didn't mind singing the songs. I enjoyed the living room soirees. I took pride in being able to speak Bengali fluently. It felt like a core part of who I was.

There were other stops too, and these were less of the brown-specific variety. Atish *loved* department stores and wholesalers. Whenever he could, he used to take us to a chain called Zellers, where he'd revel in scouring for the best deals and finding treats to buy for us. His fascination with Zellers had something to do with being an immigrant, I think. Bishakha and Atish didn't grow up around Costco, Target, Sam's Club, or Zellers. It was the kind of store where Atish could walk in and say, "Look at all this *stuff*. There's so much of it!" For someone who grew up like Atish, department stores represented the kind of largesse he had in mind when he first came to Canada.

My uncle had a particular fascination with baseball, a sport that wasn't common in India. Atish grew up with cricket. He loved throwing tennis balls to us in the narrow apartment hallway, and we'd field them with mitts on as if we were on an actual diamond. One time he took us to what was then called the

SkyDome, the home field of the Toronto Blue Jays, for a game. I ran the bases with my younger cousin Sagnik afterward as part of a promotion the franchise was throwing for kids twelve and under. As we finished our faux home-run trots, Atish was at home plate cheering us on.

Even though Atish and Sima went out of their way to spoil us, they did not live a life of luxury. Their apartment was physically small, and they were frugal with money. My aunt and uncle didn't buy clothes very often. Gifts from Atish and Sima were thoughtful but not extravagant. Instead of spending money on lavish meals, they avoided eating out when they could. This is part of the brown experience. We rarely went to sit-down restaurants growing up. In fact, if I ever tagged along with one of the adults to the mall when they went shopping, I'd repeatedly stroll by the Chinese fast food restaurant in the food court and grab samples because it was so unusual for us to eat outside the home. On the rare occasions we *did* go out to eat in Canada, there were always fights among the parents over who would pay the check. This is a common immigrant thing too: It's a point of pride to pay the bill at dinner or go above and beyond to be gracious hosts. At night, we found spaces on the living room floor to sleep. Atish snored terribly every night. It sounded like a duck was trying out for an a capella group inside his nose. But I didn't sleep much anyway, because I'd be up late with Sagnik playing the computer games I didn't have at home.

But *this* was family. For one glorious week out of the year, we weren't disjointed. We were warm, safe, and cared for. When the visits took place during the winter, I got a taste of the Christmas spirit I saw in movies. We didn't sing carols or sip eggnog, but we laughed over curries and opened gifts from Atish and Sima.

As I got older, the visits to Toronto became less frequent and then eventually stopped entirely as things got worse at home. I drifted away from Atish, Sima, and Sagnik. The more distant my relationship with my parents became, the guiltier I felt about the idea of being close with Atish and Sima. Furthermore, the two of them seemed like relics from a past life. I wasn't that kid anymore who loved sitting in their living room. The one happy thread I had tying me to my brownness gradually frayed. After the divorce, Bishakha and Shyamal lost touch with Atish too. With my father, it was a natural result of the divorce. With my mother, it was the result of a dispute involving my grandmother's property in India. Yet another casualty of the tumult.

Sattik and Erica, my sister-in-law, usually host the holidays at their cozy two-story house in Howell, and Christmas 2018 was no different. I have spent Christmas and Thanksgiving with them every year, dating back to college, unless work got in the way. My mother was rarely there, a result of her own complicated relationship with Sattik, which is why Wesley and I visited her before joining the festivities.

Holidays, in my adult years, have always been a source of conflicting emotions. I'm grateful for the strong relationship I have with Sattik. He's always been my advocate and biggest role model. I enjoy being at my brother's home with his family celebrating holidays and birthdays, but at my core, I still feel a sense of longing. The holidays are supposed to remind us of what we have and to be thankful for it. But for me, they've always been a reminder of what I lacked. Sattik had Erica and his own children. I've always felt like a distant cousin when visiting them: late to the party, accepted, but a fleeting member of the group. I take part in the traditions: sitting around the Christmas tree and exchanging gifts, sipping whiskey and watching holiday movies, the ham dinner, all of it. But many times, I've felt a sense of emptiness in these situations, as if I was a stray family member recently picked up for the ride.

That's not a reflection on Sattik and Erica, mind you. They're wonderfully welcoming, as is Erica's family. It's a reflection of how unsettled I felt in my parents' absence, even recognizing how unhappy I felt when they were there. In my twenties, I never celebrated Thanksgiving and Christmas. I *tolerated* them.

Sattik's approach to the relationship with Atish and Sima was the opposite of mine, even as he too drifted from Bishakha. He correctly recognized that they could be grandparent-like figures to his children, Tessa and Braden (then seven and four years old), and he made the effort to stay close to them even as he fell out with each of our parents. It's been important for Sattik, he told me, to re-create the experiences we had on our Toronto visits and pass them on to his children.

So there I was, after all these years, cramped on a couch with Atish and Sima, catching up around Christmas. In recent years, Atish, Sima, and Sagnik had begun making the trek down to New Jersey around the holidays.

When I walked into Sattik's house, a thirty-minute drive from my mother's apartment, I heard the familiar "HEY SHAMBO!" of my childhood. I touched Atish and Sima's feet and introduced them to Wesley.

Part of Erica's family is Italian, which means a traditional Feast of the Seven Fishes on Christmas Eve. It is easily my favorite part of the holidays: an opportunity to pig out on linguini with clams, crab cakes, fried fish, homemade lobster bisque, and whatever else. After dinner, Wesley and I quickly found ourselves in the living room so we could digest, along with my aunt and uncle. Sattik and Erica worked in the kitchen while Tessa and Braden sat near us on the floor, playing with L.O.L. dolls and Legos, desperately hoping a wayward adult would wander by to play with them. Everything had come full circle. Just as Sattik, Sagnik, and I had played on the living room floor at the feet of Atish and Sima when we were children, there were Tessa and Braden doing the same decades later. We had passed the living room torch from one generation to the next.

Atish and Sima were characteristically warm toward me, even though it had been a while since we had spoken at length. I told Atish, as we settled onto the couch, how difficult some of the recent conversations had been with Shyamal and Bishakha.

"They're different now," I said. "They're older and I think regretful."

Atish, now in his midsixties, seemed mournful in thinking about his own relationship, or lack thereof, with Bishakha.

"I hope so. You know that's how it should be. At some point in life, as long as you realize that, you know, we are all human beings, Shambo," Atish said. "I could get mad. I could get sad. We get mad. We get happy or whatever. That's how we are as human beings. And when we are mad, we say things and we do things which we regret later—but that's the key. We should not do this thing, but we should regret it and say sorry for it."

He seemed to be convincing himself of this as much as he was telling me.

"Shambo, the thing is that if you do not have peace at home, you can work hard or whatever, but you've got to have someone to come back to," Atish said. "You remember I used to watch my favorite television show, *Cheers*? And there was that song called—"

"You want to go where everybody knows your name, yeah," I interrupted.

"So this is the thing. Where you are comfortable, where you feel good: That's the thing that you guys didn't have. Like if I'm away, as soon as I get out of home, let's say fifteen minutes, I get a phone call. 'Where are you?'" Atish said, looking at Sima, his wife of more than thirty years. "Sometimes I get mad. She always worries about me. But that's the thing: I know inside that I'm wanted. That someone is missing me. Someone wants me home. So that's the thing: You have to have love in your life."

Atish had learned how to love properly, despite growing up in the same environment as Bishakha. Atish loved Sima, and vice versa. They both cared deeply about Sagnik. And Sattik and me. It was in their nature.

But as warmly as I felt toward Atish, I had some growing resentment about the situation into which Bishakha was forced during her teenage years: that she had been, essentially, exiled to Canada after the death of her father to build her own life by herself at a young age. No *wonder* she had such a difficult time as a mother, having been shoved out the door by her family. I pictured Atish and Bishakha as children. He said she was always "very jolly," which I wish I could've seen. I wondered if the two of them ever played together. Bishakha loved books: Maybe, as the two of them grew older, Bishakha read to him out loud at night. Maybe they fought and teased each other, as siblings do, happily playing again within minutes. Maybe she helped him with homework.

"Why was Mom in Canada? Who made the decision to send her?" I asked.

"That was our parents," Atish said plainly.

"So why did they send her? How did she end up going there?" I asked.

"She came here because she was married to another person at the time," he said nonchalantly.

The answer sped by me, the way a car might on a highway, and gave me whiplash. *Wait, wait, wait, wait, wait, wait. What?*

"No, no. She was in Toronto—" I protested.

"Yeah, because they came here."

"I don't understand," I said.

"That person married her, and they came here," Atish said.

"Wait, you're saying she was married to someone previously before my father?" I said, startled.

"Yeah."

It turned out that my mother had purposely skipped over a portion of her story in our discussion. She hadn't come to Canada on her own. While in India, Amiya, my grandmother, had arranged Bishakha off to another man at a very young age, around seventeen years old. Atish said he had met the man once and that Amiya had handled most of the arranging, just as she would later do with Bishakha and Shyamal. He didn't remember much else because he was so young. Atish estimated that Bishakha was married to the first husband for about three or four years. She lived with him in the United Kingdom before moving to Canada with him, where she spent her twenties. The divorce happened in Toronto soon after their arrival in Canada, from his telling.

"He was a bad, bad person," Atish said, adding, "There were stories I heard. He was abusive to her."

If you consider how terrible my parents' marriage was—and that they took decades to divorce—how bad must it have been for Bishakha's first marriage to end in a matter of years? Without realizing it, Atish had turned over a stone I hadn't even been looking for. For the first time, I saw my mother as something more than a stranger or a source of strife. She was a survivor of abuse.

I thought about what she must have gone through—not only being in an abusive relationship, but an abusive relationship that carried her over two continents where she didn't speak the language or have any family or friends. It doesn't take a professional psychologist to realize that spending several years in a distressing marriage in a strange foreign country may make you hesitant to remarry.

It would also explain why she had a difficult time connecting with my father—and her children. It would shed light on why she had trouble connecting with me.

Conclusions began to form in my mind. My experience was not just about being a brown kid in a white town. I didn't just fall out of touch with my parents because they were immigrants and couldn't relate to me. Something *happened*: a massive, unexposed trauma that unwittingly permeated my entire childhood.

And the trauma went unaddressed. For one thing, we didn't talk about emotions. We didn't have frank discussions—or any discussions—about mental health. Where many of my white friends saw therapists growing up, it wasn't the kind of treatment my family was ever open to considering—because they didn't know to consider it. In the same way that Indian parents, or at least my Indian parents, had their children solely focused on academics as opposed to social development, they didn't know how to turn the gaze inward, or even that they are supposed to. Depression, abuse, and trauma can fly into a family like meteors, leaving massive craters in their wake. But those craters come secondary to putting food on the table and making sure your children succeed on paper. I had avoided closeness with Atish out of guilt about the lack thereof with my mother, but in a sad and twisted irony, reaching out to him sooner would have bridged many of the gaps that had kept my mother and me apart.

I wasn't sure where to place the blame. My grandmother was arguably the catalyst for what happened to my mother. But she also arranged Atish's marriage to Sima in the mid-1980s, in a manner similar to Bishakha's. And that decision worked out fine. Better than fine, in fact. It couldn't have been by accident. Amiya had found in Sima a loving, desirable partner for Atish, the complete opposite result of what happened in each of Bishakha's two marriages. Atish drew the right straw while Bishakha twice got the wrong one.

The Atish and Sima connection went something like this: Amiya put an ad in the newspaper and Sima's parents, with Sima still living in India, responded on her behalf, just as Amiya had with Bishakha and Shyamal.

"It's the same thing you guys have. Whatever dating site you use," Atish said.

"Ancestry.com," Sima offered.

She meant Tinder. Or Hinge. Or Bumble. But that's not the point.

Sima met with three potential suitors, Atish being one of them. She picked my uncle. Although, from Sima's telling, this marriage was destiny. When she was young, her parents had consulted a palm reader who had written several predictions about Sima's future: One of them was that she would marry someone who lived outside of India. Atish was living in Canada. Sima didn't want to go back to Canada with him, but it was her fate.

"Maybe because I liked him?" Sima said, followed by a hearty cackle. That seemed to be the case. This arranged marriage has lasted more than three decades, and from my vantage point, their love for each other seems to have only increased.

"I must say one thing," Atish declared from the couch. "I don't know which one is right, which one is wrong, because both sides have some flaws, arranged marriage or dating marriage, whatever they do here."

Atish wagged his finger.

"I have seen dating marriages. They are dating for two years, and then they make a big announcement. They go to Hawaii, Honolulu, or Mexico, they get married. They're really in love, and then after six months, they've separated because they need some space."

Everyone in the room burst out laughing, including Sagnik, my cousin, who sat silently nearby. He's a quiet type, unlike his parents. But Atish and Sima didn't want to arrange a marriage for Sagnik, even as I teased that they should.

Atish continued: "See, this is something you have to understand, we are in a different country now. His buildup is different than ours. It's always important to have a second opinion. Sometimes when you are in love, you don't see the fault, which an experienced person can see. Maybe that way I could suggest to him. No, but I would not tell him to not marry this girl and marry that girl. No. Never."

I glanced at Sagnik, who, in contrast to my uncle, possesses a wiry frame and an unassuming demeanor. I considered that he was living the life my parents meant for Sattik and me to have, just as Ron and Trisha, the children of Shyamal's nephew Somnath, were living in Connecticut. It's the life we should've had. Sagnik was impressive: smart and a self-starter who has built a stable career for himself as an accountant. He is close to his parents, even taking care of them as they get older. He had grown up understanding and appreciating Indian culture, and he is exceedingly polite and respectful of elders. Atish, Sima, and Sagnik were the opposite of Shyamal, Bishakha, Sattik, and me. I didn't have that stability growing up, but I knew I wanted to build that life for myself with my own children. Maybe I would with Wesley.

It was getting late. Tessa and Braden were put to bed after leaving out milk and cookies for Santa. Not wanting to incur

Santa's wrath or his coal on Christmas Eve, they didn't put up a fight about going to sleep early. Sagnik, Sima, and Atish turned in for the night soon after. Wesley and I cozied up on a surprisingly comfortable sofabed.

But we lay awake, processing all the night's revelations. I had the strangest feeling, as I held Wesley close that night. It was an unfamiliar one, a slight tingle. I wasn't sure how to handle it. My body had to do some translating. As much as my mind was whirling from the revelations about Bishakha, as I closed my eyes, I couldn't help but notice that for possibly the first time since I was a child, I wasn't merely *tolerating* this time of year. With Atish, Sima, Sagnik, and Wesley nearby, as well as my brother's family, I felt a sense of warmth and I was looking forward to Christmas morning. I didn't feel adopted. I felt like I was nine again in Toronto. I felt at home.

SEVENTEEN

"I couldn't even think. I was so lost."

On New Year's Eve, Wesley and I went to the studio apartment of my friend Matt on the Upper East Side for a quiet evening. Matt and I grew up together in Howell and had celebrated every New Year's together going back to college. Some of them were big bashes at our respective schools. One was a trip to Puerto Rico. But now, both being thirty, we wanted something more relaxing. Although on this particular evening, we were so boring that we swung the pendulum too far. A coma would have been less relaxing.

Matt has long been one of my closest friends. Ever since we met in high school, we've spent multiple nights on the phone every week, just shooting the shit about anything. Movies. Television. Sports. Sometimes our phone conversations are just silent, punctuated only by grunts as we watch a basketball game. True friendship. He's always been steadfast and reliable.

Yet, strangely enough, I've never spoken much to him about my family life. The lack of talk has always been my source of comfort.

Sitting on Matt's couch as we watched television, my phone buzzed right before midnight. It was a text from my mother. She had really mastered this.

"Happy new year. And for the rest of the year.good night."

Bishakha and I had been texting more often, and about mundane things. The day before, she wrote, "Oh I am watching Obama in Oprah very nice."

Okay, she still needed some work.

But it was another text Bishakha sent shortly after receiving the first that stood out to me more than anything. It was to Wesley. After exchanging similar pleasantries with her, my mother sent one that said: "I am going to have a good year. And a new life."

Wesley and I traded looks. Her bottom lip curled. It was the first time I could remember Bishakha ever expressing any sort of optimism for the future. I think about that text often now when I'm not with her. Love and care are obviously crucial parts of a healthy family dynamic. So are trust, safety, communication. Those are the traits that first come to mind in picturing a comfortable home.

But optimism isn't a trait we discuss much. We probably should in deciding what makes a family work. The ability for a group of people to look toward the future and say, "This is something for us to look forward to" is as crucial as having good things in the present. For the first time in such a long time, my mother was sitting at home, curled up in her bed, with cell phone in hand, and sharing New Year's Eve with other people. We weren't with her but we were *with her*. She had, by her own words, a "new life," a light at the end of a dark tunnel, which happened to be coinciding with a new calendar. As the ball dropped in Times Square, my mother was turning a new page and aiming to write a new story for herself.

There was, however, one potential wrinkle. I would have to

ask my mother about her previous husband at some point, but I was nervous that it might rock the boat. I had compiled all the pieces to the puzzle but hadn't yet completed it—and I felt like I needed to. Our relationship was the best it had been in our lifetimes. I ran the risk of upsetting my mother by forcing her to bring up memories that she didn't want to confront.

But, selfishly, I also knew that I knew about her previous marriage. I needed her to know that I knew, and I needed to tell her it was okay to talk about it. If she was ashamed about it, I needed to tell her she had no reason to be. Arrogantly, I felt entitled to know about it and how it affected the rest of her life. After all, it directly affected mine.

One Sunday morning in early February, Shyamal video chatted with me and Wesley using his phone. This wasn't the first time we had tried this, by the way, since returning from India, but previous attempts weren't as successful. My father initially couldn't figure how to get his phone to shoot his face. So Wesley and I had a lovely view of his kitchen table as we spoke. Bishakha wasn't the only person who needed smartphone lessons.

When Shyamal saw Wesley's face, he chortled loudly. This time we could see his face.

"HOW ARE YOU?!" Shyamal blared, followed by, "HA, HA, HA."

We spent some time catching up. I told him about some of the pieces I had written and that Wesley and I were planning on traveling soon. Shyamal said he had suffered a wrist injury from playing tennis.

"Hey, Dad, did you know Mom was married before you?" I asked.

I went for it. No warning. No lead-up. I did not pass Go. No "*I have something I wanted to talk to you about, Dad."* I was intending on going that route, of course, but, impulsively, I skipped the preamble. What was the point? I wasn't afraid of him getting angry at me for asking the question. Maybe it was the journalist in me. If I could press politicians with difficult questions on the fly, surely I could do the same with my father. I didn't want to waste time. I needed answers. I had an internal *A Few Good Men* voice: I wanted the truth.

There was a beat of silence. The question, obviously, had caught Shyamal off guard.

"I had some idea," he said slowly.

"Did you know anything about how long it was or anything like that?" I asked.

"No."

He wouldn't say much else about it. But after a few seconds, he sagely said, "The world is not a very straightforward place."

No, it isn't. A significant portion of the South Asian experience, at least from what I have seen among brown friends and my own family members, is about *seeming* a certain way to give off the impression of stability and status, at the expense of emotional needs. It's why Bishakha, when I was little, loved telling people that I spoke fluent Bengali and sang Indian songs. I was a reflection of her effort. It was important for her to keep up the façade that we were a traditional Indian family achieving the American Dream.

There is a formula to this for many Indians: Go to school. Get good grades so you can get into another school. Get a job, preferably in what your parents want you to study. Get a better job. Get married (in many cases, how and to whom your parents want you to). Have children. Have those children do the same thing. Wash, rinse, and repeat. Everything else is unimportant or a peripheral concern. This prescription is not universal by any means, and it is becoming more flexible by the decade. I have several brown friends who experienced varying degrees of this. Some went through all of it, and others, zero. But even those who avoided the traditional brown path know many who didn't. Certainly, this dynamic was apparent with my mother and father. Empathy is a learned skill. Their mothers and fathers rarely asked, within the framework of the checklist: *Is this what you want? Will this make you happy? Will this fulfill you?* In turn, my parents never learned fully how to express empathy.

Shyamal, from what I could tell, thought Bishakha *seemed* fine when they met. Because he was checking off the box: Getting married. No one thought to ask if she *was* fine, beyond the cosmetic. Not my grandmother. Not my father or my uncle. Even knowing what she had been through, none of the people closest to her recognized the impact it had on her as a wife and a mother. Our culture, with a general aversion to placing mental health at the same level of importance as academic and professional achievement, failed Bishakha.

Weeks later, with much trepidation, I called my mother. I had to put my cards on the table. The conversation had filled me with dread for weeks, going all the way back to Christmas when I first learned about the marriage. All I wanted for Bishakha was for her to be happy. This talk would *not* make her happy.

I was going to buck traditional brownness. We were going to communicate about feelings and needs.

When Bishakha picked up the phone, she told me she had spent the weekend celebrating Saraswati Puja, an annual event honoring the Hindu goddess of knowledge.

"Mom, when you first left India, were you married once before my father?" I asked her in Bengali, to make her feel comfortable. I made sure my tone was measured and warm, in contrast to the conversation with Shyamal. I had the same fervent desire for answers but not the same appetite for directness.

Once again, there was a beat of silence, just like when I asked Shyamal.

"Yes, I did marry," Bishakha said in a low voice, barely above a murmur.

"I didn't know that. You never told me that," I said.

"It never came up. That's why. It was a long, long time ago. He left me."

It never came up. She was right about this, at least semantically. Bishakha told me that Canada was always supposed to be their final destination. But first, after the wedding (which would've been sometime in the mid-1960s), Bishakha and her husband stopped off in Manchester, England, where the husband had lived for a while. My mother fell seriously ill after somehow contracting typhoid fever and was hospitalized for at least a week. And somewhat amazingly, during most of that year in Manchester, Bishakha said she barely saw her husband. She didn't know where he was. He'd come and go from their home. They barely spoke. He didn't come visit her at the hospital.

She eventually recovered from the illness, and they moved to Canada together. My mother was around eighteen. Soon after that, he was gone. It might have been days. It might have been weeks. It was at most another two years. Her husband, whom she barely knew, packed his bags and left. She was a recent immigrant. She didn't know the language. She didn't have any friends. She didn't understand how things worked. She was alone and abandoned.

"This must have had quite an impact on you," I said.

"Yes, very much. Let me tell you, Shambo. My life is very complicated. I've always struggled. I'm so used to it."

"Did this factor into why you didn't want to marry Dad?"

"Oh, yes."

There it was. The final puzzle piece was in its place. It was the confirmation of something I had only begun piecing together around Christmas. I began to see the fully formed picture. I understood something neither of my parents could: My mother being abandoned created an obstacle neither of them seemed to understand. And neither ever did.

"I spent most of my life with your father," Bishakha said. She seemed ashamed about having been married twice.

"There's no shame. There's no embarrassment. This is a common thing. This is not a problem. Do you understand?" I said.

"No, I understand that. I don't know how to say it. I was so young. I had to struggle a lot."

"Mom, listen: If I was sixteen, and I had to go to a new country with a man I didn't know and I didn't know the language, that would affect me for my whole life."

"Of course it affected me, Babu. Very much."

I wasn't telling her anything she didn't know. It was those around her, especially those entrusted to protect her—like my grandmother—who should've known. They'd let her down. I asked her what she thought happened when her husband left.

"Sopan, I couldn't even think. I was so lost. I thought, 'What am I going to do? How will I survive?'"

Bishakha said she remembered that a Punjabi family in the area took pity on her and helped her learn to use public transportation and speak English. They also gave her money to help her get on her feet. And then she began the life she had described to me before.

I could hear her sobbing into the mouthpiece.

"I had to take care of Atish. I had to take care of Ma. I didn't have anyone to take care of me," Bishakha said.

"It's okay, Mom. This is all important. This is very important that we talk about this stuff. You've overcome quite a bit. I had no idea. I wish I did. It would've made all the difference," I said. By now we had shifted to conversing in English.

"I am very emotional right now. I don't want to cry," she said.

I told her we didn't have to talk about it, but that it was good we had. It felt cathartic. Though there were still unanswered questions I had about the specifics of their arrival in Canada, at that moment getting those answers felt peripheral.

"It's just such a remarkable story," I told my mother. "I don't think you have a proper appreciation of how much you've overcome. I hope that you do at some point. I understand it now. I didn't before, but I do now. And I certainly believe that you deserve better than you got."

"Thank you. Maybe, I don't know. One thing for sure: I tried my best to build a family."

Before we got off the phone, my mother had one last question for me.

"Are you going to write about the turkey thing?" Bishakha said, laughing. *The turkey thing?* This was what she wanted to know?

When I was about eight years old, and we were still living in Randolph, my family had a house right by this huge stretch of woods. As one might expect, various wildlife would swing by and visit our lawn. Lots of deer. Squirrels. One time, though, for whatever reason, there was a flock of turkeys. We looked out our window and saw a bunch of them hanging out on our front lawn. They stayed there for at least a couple of days.

One cloudy afternoon, I was walking down the street to play with a friend, while my mother watched me from our front step. It started drizzling, so I began jogging. And soon enough this jog turned into a terrorized *in-fear-for-my-life* sprint because some of the turkeys started chasing after me, apparently thinking I was a threat. Or they were trying to mimic me. Either way, these turkeys weren't playing, man. Considering some of the turkeys were at least my size, it is still a wonder how they never caught me.

Bishakha, sensing the threat, jetted out in her car in an attempt to disperse them—at least that's how I remember it. The turkeys stopped running on their own, but it was a brave mom moment nonetheless. That doesn't mean I've gotten over my fear of animals. Since then, I've been uncomfortable around all types, whether domesticated or in the wild. All of them. Ask the New York City pigeons that coo atop store awnings or the stray dogs lounging around Kolkata. Ask those menacing squirrels in Central Park.

To this day, *the turkey thing* remains one of my mother's favorite stories to tell about me. I don't blame her, I guess. I have the corniest phobia known to man. I'd make fun of it too.

"It was so funny," Bishakha said. "You were the talk of the town. Every time I see someone: 'Remember, Shambo was running with the turkeys!' It's funny now, but it wasn't funny back then."

Honestly, it was funny then. It's still funny now. And I was relieved that we got off the phone with something funny. But my mother probably remembers the turkey story for a different reason. Not just because of its humor or the absurd visual. So many of our stories come from a place of darkness. This was one where Bishakha got to be the unequivocal protective force she meant to be as a mother. When her young boy was in danger, she sprang into action. This one was pure.

EIGHTEEN

"Children of immigrants . . ."

When I took the stage at the Comic Strip Live in April 2019 for the second *Big Brown Comedy Hour* of the year, everything looked the same. The brick backdrop was still there, as was the green broom closet where comedians hang out before it's time to go on. Out in the darkness of the crowd, Wesley was taking pictures and chuckling.

During these shows, I always hang out in the back to watch some of the other comedians onstage. I got to see my hilarious friend Atheer Yacoub, a master of the deadpan, telling stories about being Muslim and growing up in Alabama. There was Ramy Youssef, who was test-driving material before taping a comedy special. He brought the house down like he always does. Dave Merheje, a comic whose manic demeanor onstage earned him a Netflix special, matched Ramy note for note.

Every time I've done these gigs in the past, I've been amazed at how much funnier those folks are than me.

But now they felt different, man. I was on their level. My skin didn't feel like a costume, despite the similar surroundings, and my sets didn't feel like a front. At the *Big Brown* show, I felt big and brown. And more than anything, my parents were no longer just a pretext for punchlines.

I told the story of my mother's reaction to my first crush, tapping into a well of affection that had grown for her over the last year.

"We're looked at as different, man. Immigrants. Children of immigrants," I said during the routine. I might as well have been talking about the way I viewed myself too. I saw myself for the first time as a child of immigrants, rather than one who mistakenly ended up with the wrong genetic sample. My take on brownness had shifted from sarcastic and ironic to an earnest embrace.

I told a true story about being part of the team that launched Al Jazeera America and how we were constantly told to change the name of the network, because a lot of people in the United States thought we were a terrorist group.

"No! Why should we change who we are? Why should we bend to the ignorance of other people? We are always the ones being asked to change!" I declared onstage. There wasn't a punchline for that one.

One day, I told the crowd, I was outside of St. Malachy's Church, in New York's theater district, shooting exteriors as part of a feature we were doing on the chapel. An older white guy came up to us and asked what we were doing. I told him about the story we were working on and that it was for Al Jazeera America.

"Oh, Al Jazeera. Nice to see you guys doing something peaceful for once."

The audience got a good laugh out of that.

I added, "Not with that attitude!" while scrunching into the microphone.

When I walked off the stage, I felt funny. *Actually funny.* As in the way a comedian is supposed to feel when they finish a set.

Following the first *Big Brown* show of the year, which was early in the winter, I got some unexpected external validation on my way out the door. An older brown woman, who looked to be in her fifties, came up to me in the lobby after the show.

"I've seen you before," she said sternly. "You've gotten much better." Then she strolled away without another word. A true brown moment, where even a compliment feels like a criticism.

This time it was Wesley who was standing by the front door, ready to offer me my validation. When I finally snaked my way around the throngs of people headed for the exit, I saw that Ron, Susmita and Somnath's son, was standing next to her. He was just finishing college *after* managing a successful state representative campaign. This was the latest of several instances in which Ron had come down from Connecticut to visit. Sometimes he needed a place to stay if he was interviewing for a job or had an event to attend. I've even had the opportunity to offer him advice. "From an older Deb to a younger Deb," I once said to him before catching myself. "I've never had the chance to say that before!"

Ron was the first family member to come see me perform in person other than my brother, Sattik. I was relieved that the Comic Strip show went so well because the first set of mine he saw could not have been worse. We dragged him to Brooklyn on a freezing night for a show called *Bushwick Bears* well before the Comic Strip show. Every single joke bombed. Even a newsy joke I had written for that night was met with such silence that I had to follow up with, "So nobody heard about this?" In the immediate aftermath of walking off the stage, I vowed never to do comedy ever again, which sometimes happens. Ever the politico, Ron gamely said he enjoyed himself.

While I was heartened by the new Deb family member in attendance, I felt the absence of an older member of the lineage who wasn't. I wished Shyamal was there. He was, of course, still in India. I knew he wouldn't have understood any of the jokes and would probably have clapped in all the wrong places, but he would have been so excited nonetheless. No, he would have been proud.

My father wasn't totally absent from the evening, though. I had accidentally given him a taste of my comedic stylings the afternoon before the show. See, I typically write out my set before each show because I like to have notes to go over before I hit the stage. Then I'll email them to myself.

Except this time, when I walked inside the club, I noticed the email wasn't in my inbox. Digging around in my sent messages, I found that Shyamal—not Sopan—had received my set notes. Until this point, my father had a minimal idea of what my comedy is all about. Of course, this set featured plenty of material about my parents, including the story about Shyamal finding out about my arrest from newspapers in India.

I was literally sweating. I didn't know what he'd think. I was worried he'd be offended. I feverishly tapped out a follow-up email.

"Haha baba please ignore this email I was prepping for a show."

Six hours later, he responded: "I read it and I liked it."

Phew.

That's when the pang of longing hit me. I wanted him to be watching in the audience instead of reading a summary thousands of miles away. *I've missed my father.* I don't know that I've ever said that in my life. Because it was never true before. I missed his cackle, the hand gestures and his "*No, no, no, no, no.*" I even missed standing in the heat wearing a plastered smile while he snapped pictures with his point-and-shoot camera.

But Shyamal won't be seeing my comedy in person anytime

soon. He might come and visit us someday, but he'll never live in the United States again. I've come to terms with the life Shyamal has built in India. He's at peace. My father has his routines. He has his tennis matches, a cozy flat, his paintings, a thirst for travel, and the security of knowing that he's lived the last dozen years on his own terms.

And still, I hear the sadness in his voice. My father called me near the start of the New Year to tell me he had taken a trip to Puri, the beach city where Bishakha's father died. Shyamal excitedly told me about the bird sanctuary he had visited. Even though he seemed like his energetic self in describing his day, I sensed his desire for companionship in the tone of his voice. He was alone. There was the hint of emptiness, as if he was straining to put up a front. My father could only share the experience with me from a distance. But that's something. He told me he would send me pictures from the trip. I told him I would send him pictures from stand-up.

My mother hasn't been in the city to see me perform yet either, but both of my parents are more active parts of the life Wesley and I lead. They treat Wesley as if she is another daughter, and she treats them as surrogate parents. My parents seem happier now. After a lifetime of sadness, they are entitled to at least that much. They shouldn't have the bar set simply to "survival." In the last year, I'd like to think I've raised it just a little.

My brother said it best to me recently: "Ultimately, it's about forgiveness." Until Sattik put it that way, I hadn't consciously considered how deeply bitter and angry I still was about my relationship with my parents before reaching out to them. It wasn't just that I had become estranged from them; they were genuinely sources of anger. I thought that as I grew older, the anger had passively shifted to ambivalence. But the outward ambivalence was just how my frustration, which had been building since childhood, exhibited itself. Spending time with my mother and father, from the idle chitchat to the structured interviews, revealed their humanity. And learning about the culture that birthed Shyamal and Bishakha allowed for an absolution to take place. I learned the context for their flaws. Their sadness pained me—independent of its impact on my life. And I can't be angry anymore. I have to let go.

Without the tumult of our past, I am not sure if my parents and I would be in a better place or just a more neutral one. I am not sure if I would be in a better place. The knot of emotion inextricably linked to the fires of my childhood made washing that pain away feel euphoric.

We all failed, in our own way. Draw a line between any two members of the Deb family and you'll find a long history of could've-done-betters. Even now, my parents have failed to forgive each other, and Bishakha and I have found it challenging to find fully solid ground. I still have resentment about my father leaving the country without warning. But this was never supposed to be a one-step process, and I can be grateful nonetheless for how far we've come. What is light without darkness? I'm grateful when my phone rings and Shyamal is shouting "BABA!" on the other end, or when an excessively Scotch-taped holiday card arrives from my mother. Wesley and I can be grateful for each other, both having seen the holes that rocky relationships can leave.

And now that both parents are more active parts of my life, I get to say to them: *I've seen you before. You've gotten much better.*

Sattik was right: forgiveness *was* at the core of this. And it wasn't just my own. The Deb family was like a web with new threads popping up all over the place. That trip my mother took to India where she picked up rubies for Wesley's engagement ring? Bishakha had a tearful reunion in Kolkata with Siddhartha and Meera, my aunt and uncle, and they are now in semi-regular contact. Somnath and Susmita have welcomed Wesley and me to their home in Connecticut. Ron has even met Wesley's brother, Ansel, and bonded over a shared fascination with religion. Atish and Sima are back in my life as a welcome second set of parents. The Hindu figurines that my aunt gave us as part of the blessing ceremony in India hold a prominent place in our bedroom.

Somnath has encouraged me to remember that we are all imperfect in our own ways, my mother and father included, and we can't fully understand each other's struggles. I never understood the burden my mother carried, keeping a trauma secret while trying to build a life beyond it. Where I only remember my father's disappearance to India, Somnath remembers the lonely, helpless man he was before he left.

"Your dad didn't abandon you," he told me. "He hung in there and took care of you in his limited and flawed way until you left home and went to college. But he was dying from the inside. There was no medical miracle waiting for him in India. He was emotionally devastated in the United States, but he healed from the inside with his family's support in India."

I asked myself repeatedly at the beginning of all this: Is it too late to try this? Is there a point? We are who we are, right? I can now say with resounding force that it was not too late. We are who we are, and now I know who that is.

All it took was the premise of my first-ever joke, that first time I made people laugh from the backseat of a car as a young boy. It was what inspired me to pursue laughter from an audience wherever I could for as long as I could. And it was about my parents getting lost.

I had to turn a shortcut into a long cut.

EPILOGUE

Both of my parents, in the last year, have begun keeping Wesley and me in the loop about their day-to-day lives. One email I received from Shyamal in the fall detailed a safari trip to Madhya Pradesh, a state in central India. "Though we visited two safaris, all we could see a tiger for was three seconds," my father wrote. Shyamal's life was an adventure. I don't think he'd have it any other way.

And my mother sent her own updates. In the winter, she wrote, "Hi shambo, How did you and wesley survive the weather? In here it was really Very bad. Did you go to work? Stay worm."

Stay worm. That made me laugh.

I sent both parents early copies of this book in manuscript format. Shyamal's response was so brilliantly Shyamal.

You have done a wonderful job as a journalist. I am very proud of you. This book may reunite this family and your parents can spend the remaining few years of their lives in peace. I shall start writing a book of my own 'The Untold Story—My life.' soon. I shall take your help on that.

Of course, Dad. Whatever you need.

The road for my mother and I, on the other hand, has not always been smooth. But that's okay. I imagine that seeing my feelings about my upbringing in print was difficult for her. But I was lifted by a note she sent while reading an early chapter:

I am getting to know you more. There is so many things in my mind I wanted to tell you. But always remember I love you, no matter what.

ACKNOWLEDGMENTS

This has been an intensely personal project that would not have come together if not for the generous support of friends, colleagues, strangers, and family. Nothing has been more difficult and, at the same time, more exhilarating.

My everlasting gratitude goes to the book's editor, Matthew Daddona, and the team at Dey Street. You doggedly pushed me to be better and never settle, and I am eternally grateful.

To the team at CAA: Jeff Jacobs, David Larabell, and Ali Spiesman, all of whom believed in the project early on, helped shape it, and wholeheartedly encouraged me to pursue it.

To Hasan Minhaj, seeing your Netflix special, *Homecoming King*, was a seminal moment for me and many other brown people. It inspired me to share my story. Thank you for your support.

To my mother and father, both of whom were so generous with their time and effort in sharing their stories. And to my brother, Sattik, for his warmth and influence throughout my life. Further thanks to my extended family for their magnamity throughout the process: Atish, Sima, Sagnik, Susmita, Somnath, Ron, Trisha, and my aunts and uncles in India—Sudhirendra, Namita, Siddhartha, and Meera.

To Dean Obeidallah and Maysoon Zayid, for creating a space for brown comedians like *The Big Brown Comedy Hour*—and for booking me.

There are several brown comedians, writers, and actors who are my inspirations and who set the stage for me to tell my story: Kumail Nanjiani, Kal Penn, Aparna Nancherla, Russell Peters, Hari Kondabolu, Aasif Mandvi, Mindy Kaling, Jhumpa Lahiri, and many others. Without the hard work and all you overcame in your respective careers, this book wouldn't exist.

To Steve Chaggaris, for strenuously fact-checking the book.

To friends like Eli Stokols and Matt Stein, who were not just reliable confidants but excellent early readers.

To Priya Arora, Dr. Haimanti Roy, and Soné Anandpara, for the immensely helpful feedback.

To Manvi Goel and Jayanth Jagalur Mohan, for inviting us to their wedding and providing the nudge I needed for this project.

To Julie LaRue and Myriam Dietrich, for being marvelous proofreaders and raising such a wonderful human.

And, of course, to Wesley: You were a second writer, proofreader, fact-checker, and amazing travel partner. I wouldn't be here without you.

ABOUT THE AUTHOR

Sopan Deb is a writer for the *New York Times* where he has covered culture and basketball. He is also a New York City–based comedian. Before joining the *Times*, Deb was one of a handful of reporters who covered Donald Trump's presidential campaign from start to finish as a campaign embed for CBS News. He covered hundreds of rallies in more than forty states for a year and a half and was named a "breakout media star" of the election by Politico.

At the *New York Times*, Deb has interviewed high-profile subjects such as Denzel Washington, Stephen Colbert, the cast of *Arrested Development*, Kyrie Irving, and Bill Murray. Deb's work has previously appeared on NBC, Al Jazeera America, and in the *Boston Globe*, ranging from examining the trek of endangered manatees to following a class of blind filmmakers in Boston led by the former executive producer of *Friends*. He won an Edward R. Murrow award for *Larger Than Life*, a documentary he produced for the *Boston Globe*, which told the story of NBA Hall of Famer Bill Russell's complicated relationship with the city of Boston.

He lives in New York City with his fiancée, Wesley.